A Home Cook's Guide

By Albert L. Swope

Copyright

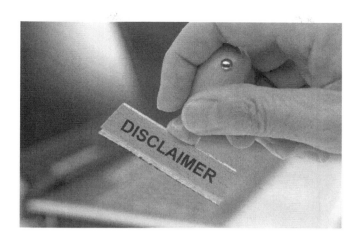

Disclaimer

An effort has been made to present accurate, up to date, reliable, complete information. However, No warranty whatsoever is being expressed or implied regarding the contents of this book.

By reading this book, readers acknowledge that the author is not rendering professional advice of any kind about any subject.

By reading this book, the reader agrees that the author has no responsibility for losses, direct or indirect, which may be incurred as a result of the use of the information in this book, including, but not limited to, errors, omissions, or inaccuracies.

Table of Contents

Introduction

Yogurt has been part of our diet for hundreds of years. It is incredibly nutritious and has numerous health benefits. The bacteria for making yogurt are known as cultures that react with lactose, the natural sugar found in fresh milk. You can buy different types of yogurt made from all types of milk.

Varieties include skimmed milk, semi-skimmed milk, and whole fat milk. Plain yogurt is a thick white liquid with a tangy flavor. Regular consumption has been found to reduce the risk of heart disease and osteoporosis. Some types of yogurt contain probiotics that aid digestion and reduce bloating and diarrhea. Natural yogurt also contains high levels of protein, vitamins, and minerals that are accredited with boosting immunity and helping to prevent certain illnesses.

So, Why Should You Make Your Yogurt When You Can Buy it From the Store?

The bottom line is that when you make your own yogurt, you know what you are getting. Store-bought yogurt can appear to be healthy but may contain all manner of unacceptable ingredients.

Consider these popular brands that are less healthy than ice cream.

Activia Crunchy and Creamy Strawberry Yogurt

This product contains quite a few weird ingredients. Carmine (for color) is in the top half of the list of ingredients and is made from the powdered scales of insects boiled in ammonia. The solution is then added to carminic acid, which creates carmine, a red salt used for coloring foodstuff. Sounds yummy, right?

Danone Light and Fit Cherry Yogurt

This product sounds healthy and nutritious but is filled with some disturbing ingredients, including:

- Kosher gelatin: Animal-based gelatin is not acceptable, healthy yogurts are made with pectin
- Caramel Color: Linked to cancer and found in soda
- Aspartame: artificial sweetener: Linked to headaches, depression, and ADHD
- Sucralose
- Sodium citrate

Of course, there are organic yogurts available, but they can be expensive. Making your own natural yogurt will prove a lot cheaper, as well as incredibly satisfying.

Chapter 1: History and Description

Before delving into the practical and technical aspects of preparing yogurt at home, you need to learn about its origin and composition. So, let's start by talking about its history and description, and take a look at some facts and details.

History of Yogurt

Yogurt is, interestingly, one of the oldest food items known to humankind. The birth of yogurt dates back to between 10,000 to 5,000 BCE. The word 'yogurt' is derived from the Turkish word 'yogurmak' (which means the act of curdling or thickening) and is also commonly spelled as yogourt or yogurt. It is believed that yogurt was discovered in the Neolithic period when people stored milk in pots, and it soured and curdled naturally due to high temperature.

In the Middle East, herdsmen transported milk in bags made of animal gut, which led to the curdling of milk due to its contact with the animal's intestinal enzymes. This made storage and transportation of the milk much easier. It was highly used in Mediterranean cuisine around 800 BCE, along with being an important part of the Roman and Greek cuisines.

The army of Genghis Khan in Mongolia was fed yogurt regularly in the 12th and 13th centuries because it was believed that yogurt gave them more power and promoted wellness and bravery. It was then used in the 16th century in Western Europe when a Turkish doctor prescribed yogurt for François I as a treatment for diarrhea. The 20th century witnessed the first production of yogurt for commercial use, with the first factory established in 1932 in France.

Known by various names around the globe, yogurt has now become a standard household product that's used in a lot of meals, whether it's savory or sweet. Yogurt sales have dramatically risen in the past five to seven years, witnessing a 10% increase in total.

What Is Yogurt?

Yogurt is simply a by-product of fermented milk with the help of a specific set of microorganisms, namely Lactobacillus delbrueckii subsp. bulgaricus and Streptococcus thermophilus. It forms into a thick curd that is white and creamy and can be eaten in its natural form or used as an ingredient in cooking.

How Is It Made?

Plants and factories that specialize in making yogurt produce a large scale daily. There are a lot of different processes and ways of manufacturing various kinds of yogurts. But let's understand the most basic and standard method of preparing the ordinary kind, to get a clearer picture. These are the crucial steps involved in the process:

Standardization and Homogenization

This is the first stage of making yogurt. A quantity of raw milk is ordered from farms. This milk isn't entirely fit to convert into yogurt immediately. And thus, it undergoes some processes at the initial stage, namely standardization, pasteurization, and homogenization.

- Homogenization emulsifies the milk to keep the fat intact and to prevent it from splitting into the cream.
- Pasteurization kills harmful pathogens by heating the milk at around 176°F.
- Standardization is used to separate the dry matter from the milk.

Fermentation

This process is crucial as it involves adding the two types of bacteria, Lactobacillus delbrueckii subsp. bulgaricus and Streptococcus thermophilus, to help in fermentation. After the first stage of treating the milk, it is allowed to cool until it reaches a temperature of around 109°F to 115°F. After it has cooled, approximately 2% of the culture (lactic acid bacteria used for fermentation) is added to the milk. This specific type of yogurt culture is preferred as it gives the best flavor and texture, and it's known for its health benefits.

Storage and Packaging

Before it goes through the final packaging, other ingredients such as sugar or flavors are added to produce different types of yogurt, depending on the range of products. It is then fully allowed to cool at a temperature of 41°F and packaged for commercial selling.

Health Benefits of Yogurt

Apart from a healthy gut and proper digestion, yogurt provides many health benefits. One of the most important ones among them is the presence of probiotics. These are a certain kind of bacteria that aid in making your digestive system healthier and boosting your immune system. People who eat yogurt regularly have notably reduced problems of constipation, gas, bloating, and diarrhea due to the presence of probiotics in it. It also increases the absorption of essential nutrients from your food, such as vitamins and minerals. Along with this, it helps to maintain body weight. Yogurt also contains calcium, which is beneficial for your teeth and bones, as well as keeping your blood pressure balanced and promoting faster healing of wounds.

Chapter 2: Different Types of Milk Yogurt Made Around the World

People often weigh the quality of yogurt based on the culture that's used to prepare it. In reality, it's not the culture that matters but the type of milk that's used. Almost all regions around the world have a specialized type of yogurt. The resultant yogurt also differs in texture and thickness.

The most common yogurt types are made of whole cow's milk. However, there are other types of milk commercially available in today's market. These alternative kinds of milk may, however, differ in fat quantity, along with the consistency in thickness and texture.

Cow's Milk Types

This is the most commonly manufactured and widely consumed yogurt around the world. Since cow's milk is readily available in every region at an affordable price, you can easily make this kind of yogurt at home. In this section, we'll cover all the major types of cow's milk to learn the differences and choose one that suits your needs.

Whole Milk

Whole-milk yogurt is the creamiest and richest yogurt among all types made of cow's milk. It contains a high-fat content (around 8 grams in an 8-ounce glass of milk) and a rich calorie count (150 calories in an 8-ounce glass). The resultant yogurt is of the best quality and texture and is considered a great option for eating raw. Although the fat content is high in this type (making up to 12% of the daily value), a few studies show that dairy fat could actually be beneficial for the body. Even though there's not enough scientific evidence to back this up so far, you can still enjoy the taste and texture of whole-milk yogurt.

Media Crema (Table Cream)

Media Crema is condensed light cream commonly used in Latin American cooking. Media Crema mostly comes in cans, so if your local grocer doesn't carry Media Crema, you may want to find your local Latin grocery store.

Half-and-Half

Half-and-half milk yogurt refers to the kind in which half of the overall portion is made of cream and half of milk. It's also commonly known as single cream or half cream. Compared to traditional milk, it has a higher fat content, but definitely lower than full cream. To make Half-and-half at home, you can just mix ½ cup of milk and ½ cup of cream, and use it to prepare yogurt with the traditional home method (we'll talk about this in detail in the following chapters). One tablespoon of half-and-half yogurt consists of

18 calories, 1.5 grams of total fat, and 0.5 grams of protein. People also use melted butter in place of cream, but we should refrain from doing that to get denser yogurt.

2% Milk

This kind of milk simply refers to low-fat milk. It is, however, still rich in nutrition. With around 8 grams of protein and 122 calories in one cup, this type of milk is still ideal for producing rich yogurt that's nutritious. It's recommended for people who are trying to switch to healthier options with fewer calories. As compared to whole milk, this kind differs in calorie count by around 24 calories. It's high in essential nutrients such as vitamin D, vitamin B12, calcium, riboflavin, potassium, and phosphorus. However, the protein content in whole milk and 2% milk is almost the same, making it a good option for people who are trying to build muscles and reduce fat.

1% Milk

Also known as low-fat milk, 1% milk contains only 100 calories and 2.5 grams of fat in an 8-ounce glass. The main difference between 2% milk and 1% milk is the amount of reduced-fat. It is preferred by people who are trying to lose weight but don't want to cut back on dairy products. However, similar to 2% milk, this type is also high in protein with a quantity of 8 grams in an 8-ounce glass. The resultant yogurt isn't as creamy as whole-milk yogurt but is healthier and nutritious.

Skimmed Milk

Skimmed milk has the lowest percentage of fat content as compared to the three types we've listed before. It's also known as fat-free milk, but it's high in nutritional value and protein content. The yogurt prepared from this type of milk isn't really as rich in texture as whole-milk yogurt or 2%- and 1%-milk yogurt, but is extremely healthy. An 8-ounce glass of milk contains just 80 calories, making it extremely preferable for people who are trying to lose weight. People often believe that skimmed milk contains water to get its thin consistency and to reduce fat content, but that's not actually true. The thin consistency of skim milk and the yogurt made from it is only due to a low percentage of fat content present in it.

Evaporated Milk

Evaporated milk is basically heated milk that's separated from its water content. The resultant milk is creamier in taste and gets a different color. Like fresh milk, evaporated milk is high in nutrition, too. It contains essential nutrients such as calcium, protein, vitamin A, and vitamin D. If you want to avoid the hassle of preparing evaporated milk at home to make yogurt, you can buy it in canned form from any grocery store. People usually add a dash of 2% milk to it to make richer and creamier yogurt due to the lower fat content in evaporated milk.

Sweetened Condensed Milk

Sweetened condensed milk is used in countries like Vietnam to produce yogurt. It's easy to prepare and has a sweet taste. However, to make yogurt out of sweetened condensed milk, you would need some fresh yogurt for it to set. To make this, you need to add one can of sweetened condensed milk to two cans of hot water, one can of room-temperature water, and ½ to one can of fresh, traditional yogurt. Strain the mixture to smoothen its texture and store it in glass jars or plastic containers of your preference. Seal with lids or aluminum foil and put them in a big pot. Pour hot water in the pot in a way that it doesn't reach the rim of the containers and let it sit for a while. This incubation process should work within six hours, after which you'll have creamy, sweet yogurt. It works well with fruits like berries, bananas, and peaches.

Lactose-Free Milk

With the advent of newer technologies, you can now consume your favorite dairy products without experiencing negative reactions. Lactose-free yogurt is made of cow's milk that's been treated to literally be 'lactose-free' by eliminating the milk sugar and lactose that's present in it. You can hardly differentiate between the taste of normal yogurt and lactose-free yogurt. Also, it's high in essential nutrients such as calcium, protein, and probiotics.

Powdered Milk

Powdered milk is often less preferred if you want the resultant yogurt to be rich and creamy. The powdered substance doesn't really help in the fermentation process because it's overly processed or has artificial preservatives and additives. It is also often avoided due to its unpleasant taste. However, the taste subsides when it is converted into yogurt. You must check all the brands before trying to make yogurt with it as each has a different taste, and the results might vary. You might also require a small quantity of fresh yogurt to let it ferment. Unless it's an emergency, we'd recommend using natural milk instead of powdered milk.

Other Animals' Milk

Yogurt made from other animals' milk is rare and rather region-specific. We have mostly been producing and consuming products made from cow's milk because it is abundantly available everywhere in the world. But why don't we consider using milk produced by other mammals? It's because it's not widely available, isn't udder-free, and these animals can be difficult to milk. Also, the taste and texture can be quite pungent or fatty. However, there are a few animals that produce milk that's suitable for converting into dairy products such as cheese and yogurt. Let's discuss a few of them that give milk to produce rich and nutritional yogurt.

Goat's Milk

Now, we all know a few people who prefer consuming goat cheese to normal cow's milk cheese due to certain allergies or reactions. It's the same case with goat's milk yogurt, as well. According to one study, the majority of infants can easily consume goat's milk without a reaction as opposed to cow's milk.

Even though the taste might be a bit odd, goat's milk yogurt is still rich and creamy, giving you the desired texture with a relatively higher fat content. You either hate it or love it. But once you develop a taste for goat's milk yogurt, you'd always go back for more.

Sheep's Milk

With a heavier fat content as compared to traditional yogurt, sheep's milk yogurt is one type that doesn't disappoint in taste like goat's milk yogurt, and it has a richer texture. If you're reactive to cow's milk yogurt, you seriously need to consider this type to get almost the same taste and avoid allergies. It's also high in nutrition with essential components such as vitamin B, riboflavin, and calcium. A major benefit of using sheep's milk yogurt is that it keeps its consistency even during cooking without breaking down. It's highly preferred due to its sweet taste.

Mare's Milk

Mare's milk is extracted from female horses and is highly used in Europe. It is extracted when the female horses are lactating. A few studies show that the nutritional composition of mare's milk is almost similar to human milk. Its nutritional composition is high in whey protein, vitamin C, and polyunsaturated fatty acids. Yogurt made of mare's milk has a higher nutritional value and is considered healthier. Mare's milk contains antibacterial and anti-inflammatory properties that help treat allergies and skin issues. It's also much higher in protein content as compared to cow's milk. This type of yogurt is a better choice for people who are watching their weight as it contains lower fat content and calories in general.

Reindeer's Milk

Reindeer's milk can be extremely difficult to fetch, as it can only be found in the Nordic regions such as Finland and Norway, or the northern parts of Canada, Alaska, and Siberia. Even if you live in any of these regions, it can still be difficult to get reindeer's milk as milking this animal is hard and takes two people. This milk has a rich butterfat content (almost 22.5%), which makes the resultant yogurt extra creamy and rich in texture. Also, it's higher in protein and calcium content, which makes it healthier and more desirable. We highly recommend trying or making reindeer yogurt whenever you visit these regions.

Water Buffalo's Milk

Yogurt made from water buffalo's milk is simply exceptional. The butterfat content in this type of milk is much higher than that of traditional cow's milk. This makes the yogurt creamier and denser in texture. It tastes a bit sweeter as compared to cow's milk, with a touch of tang. Depending on the region you live in, it can be difficult to find water buffalo's milk. But if you do, you must try making yogurt out of it. Surprisingly, this type of yogurt is lower in cholesterol count as compared to cow's milk, even though it's higher in fat.

With a higher protein and calcium count, it's also more nutritious. An important component that is uniquely present in this milk is tocopherol, which provides antioxidant properties. Basically, yogurt made of this milk is an overall winner in categories like taste, texture, and nutrition. This concept has recently become widespread all around the world, and you can now find water buffalo's milk yogurt in large-scale grocery stores.

Now, let's take a look at the substitutes for milk in the following chapter, in case you're vegan or lactose intolerant.

Chapter 3: Different Milk Substitutes for Making Yogurt

Plant-based dairy is a healthy alternative for traditional milk-based products for people who are trying to eliminate dairy from their diets, those who are turning to vegan diets, or those who suffer from PKU or milk allergies. The culturing process with non-dairy alternatives can be tricky due to the difference in compositions and processed additives. So, it's best to choose organic milk substitutes that don't contain added preservatives. Also, you need to use a new starter with every alternative, and every time you make yogurt with these options because the process of culturing is difficult due to the absence of dairy milk properties. However, it's not impossible.

With the rising stress levels in everyday life, people are switching to healthier food choices, which has been realized within the yogurt industry. You can find a lot of alternatives for milk yogurts today in supermarkets. The most common yogurt types among those are made with soymilk, almond milk, rice milk, and fruit milk. While some people still prefer traditional cow's milk yogurt for the authentic taste, a few have become used to the taste of these healthy substitutes. Read on to discover the various alternatives for the traditional milk used to produce yogurt.

Soymilk

Soymilk is the most common alternative for dairy milk. Yogurt made from soymilk is commonly known as soy yogurt, Yofu, or Soygurt. The processing is carried out traditionally by adding the bacteria culture used for general fermentation. At times, manufacturers prefer to add sweeteners like sugar, fructose, and glucose to enhance the taste. Vegans and ovo-vegetarians are increasingly seeking soy yogurt to replenish basic yogurt needs and for nutrition. The protein count in soymilk is almost equal to cow's milk yogurt, and it's a great source of unsaturated fats. This product is also suitable for people suffering from diabetes, as it can help in lowering blood sugar levels.

To get the most out of the health properties of soy yogurt, we recommend making it at home using unsweetened soymilk. However, it can take some time to get accustomed to the beany taste of homemade soy yogurt.

Rice Milk

Rice milk is, as you guessed, made from rice. It's basically prepared with brown rice and brown rice syrup, with artificial flavors and additives. It is high in nutritional value and comprises essential components such as protein, calcium, iron, vitamin B12 and Vitamin D. It is, however, extremely low in fat content and isn't a favorite as an alternative for cow's milk to prepare yogurt. Compared to cow's milk, it is high in carbohydrate content and low in calcium. Folks who are allergic to cow's milk and soymilk or suffering from lactose intolerance may prefer yogurt made out of rice milk.

To avoid preservatives, you can make rice milk and rice milk yogurt at home. Just boil brown rice in lots of water, blend it, and filter to gain rice milk. You can then make rice milk yogurt following the traditional method.

Fruit Milk

Fruit milk can be made of practically any fruit of your choice. It's basically the pulp of fresh fruit mixed with a small quantity of condensed milk or evaporated milk. To make it, you'll first need some fruit such as mangoes, apples, avocados, bananas, peaches, or berries. Along with this, you'll need 6 ½ cups of water; one can of evaporated or condensed milk of your preference, one teaspoon of vanilla essence, and four tablespoons of sugar (optional). Scrape the fruit until you obtain a sufficient amount of pulp out of it, and mix the rest of the ingredients. You can use this as a refreshment, for desserts, or to make yogurt.

To make fruit milk yogurt, you'll additionally need a yogurt starter for the culturing process. The process would be similar to the traditional method, but it's advisable to prepare the fruit puree separately and heat it after mixing in the milk.

Nut Milk

Compared to cow's milk yogurt, nut milk yogurt is low in protein (almost by 4 to 6 grams) and calcium content. However, it is also lower in sugar content. You can find a lot of flavored almond milk yogurts in supermarkets, but you can make it at home to avoid the long list of unhealthy preservatives and additives in these commercial products. But before consuming almond milk yogurt, you need to be absolutely sure if you're allergic or not.

Another popular nut milk that's converted into yogurt is cashew milk. Compared to its counterparts, cashew milk yogurt has lower sugar content (1 gram per serving), carries fewer additives and preservatives, and provides good bacteria for gut health. However, again, it's a low source of protein (only 3 grams) and calcium, so cashew milk yogurt may not be the best for someone who is looking for high nutritional value.

Substituting plant-based dairy for normal dairy is a good idea when you have to follow precautions or are trying to eliminate dairy. We would, however, not recommend it if you want to gain high nutritional value from your yogurt without compromising on the taste and texture.

Chapter 4: Preparing the Milk and Important Temperatures

We talked about the authentic method of preparing raw milk and treating it to make yogurt in the previous chapters. Still, it's essential to dig deeper and understand all processes thoroughly. The basic steps involved in turning raw milk into yogurt involve:

- homogenization,
- pasteurization,

- sanitization by heating or boiling the milk,
- fermentation, and
- incubation.

These steps suggest that the resultant yogurt is safe to use and processed perfectly.

Let's discuss these steps again, but in further detail, also paying attention to the essential temperatures at each stage.

Homogenization

Homogenization is when the fat molecules in the milk are broken down to keep them intact and not separate to form cream. It also helps in keeping the milk's texture and color. At times, while using milk, you might notice a layer of cream on it. The fat that is present in the milk accumulates as cream when not homogenized. How this works is that the fat molecules are reduced to extremely tiny particles and spread throughout the liquid volume. The milk is passed through a minute orifice that reduces the diameter of the molecules and increases their surface area. This leads to the even distribution of fat molecules throughout the milk.

Main Stages of the Treatment of Milk

• Before the process, the fat molecules measure around 1-10 microns in size. When the milk is passed through several tiny holes, the flow is kept even, and pressure is increased. The average pressure that the milk undergoes is around 2,000-3,000 pounds per square inch.

• While this process goes on and the molecules are divided into smaller fragments, these might contain a protein layer on their edges, mostly whey and casein. The second stage helps in breaking the assembly of the protein in the milk molecules.

The ideal temperature at which homogenization takes place is between 149°F and 160°F.

Pasteurization

Pasteurization is the process of killing all harmful microorganisms in the milk, making it fit for drinking or for use in making other dairy products. Consuming raw milk can lead to various sicknesses and health issues, so countries like the United States have adopted pasteurization as a necessity before selling milk on a commercial scale. This process doesn't destroy the nutritional value of the milk and keeps it safe for consumption. A few people still believe in the goodness and benefits provided by raw milk and stick to it. However, all registered dieticians oppose it and suggest using pasteurized milk in all cases.

How pasteurization works is that raw milk is passed through stainless steel plates that are heated and up to a temperature of 161°F and processed for around 15 seconds. It's then immediately cooled down at a temperature of 39°F. During this process, the next batch of cold and raw milk is heated using the heat generated from the previously processed batch and cooled down using the cold milk. The pasteurized milk is intact with almost all the important minerals and nutrients such as vitamin A, vitamin B12, vitamin D, niacin, protein, riboflavin, potassium, phosphorus, and calcium.

Should you boil your milk to make your yogurt?

The correct answer to this question is, it depends. There are a couple of things that should be considered: The first is the desired texture of your yogurt, and the second is whether you are using raw or pasteurized milk you're using to make your yogurt. Also, it's easy to get distracted and scorch your milk, which does not improve the flavor.

The texture of your yogurt

Boiling and cooling your milk before making yogurt does, in some people's opinion, improve the feel of your homegrown yogurt. I have not found this untrue even though I've seen much literature about it. I think it's the quality of the milk product and the yogurt culture to use to make your yogurt, which has the most significant impact on the texture of your yogurt. Using milk with plenty of solids will reduce the amount of waste liquid produced by the yogurt culture and, therefore, the overall bitterness of the yogurt product. Much the same thing for the yogurt culture, not all yogurt cultures are equal. So, find a good yogurt culture that you like and stick with it. Choosing the best yogurt culture for you may require some experimentation with different cultures before you settle on your final choice.

The milk you use to create your yogurt

These days there are several milk products and milk substitute products to choose from to make your yogurt, but when working with real milk, it breaks down into two categories: pasteurize and raw.

Pasteurized Mild

Pasteurized milk has already been heat-treated, so there is no real need to boil the milk to start your yogurt. Using thick milk, such as fat-free half-and-half to enrich your milk, can add significantly to the density and creaminess of your final yogurt. To make yogurt from pasteurized milk, just, bring it to room temperature, add your culture, and give it a little time to bloom, then you can add it to your yogurt warmer or wherever you keep your temperature constant to allow your yogurt culture to mature.

Raw Milk

Raw milk must be boiled or home pasteurized for food safety reasons. There are many hazards when working with raw milk, which is why when its distributed for commercial use, milk is pasteurized. Some of those health hazards, such as E. coli, can be fatal. So, whenever you work with raw milk, you should bring it to a slow boil for about five minutes; then let it cool. Once cool, add your culture, and give it a little time to bloom, then you can add it to your yogurt warmer or wherever you keep your temperature constant to allow your yogurt culture to mature.

Home pasteurization

Home pasteurization involves using a lower temperature than boiling. Home pasteurization does take longer, and attention must be paid to maintaining the appropriate temperature throughout the process. For best results, raw milk must be heated slowly during pasteurization. Use a double-boiler. To do this:

Stovetop method

*   Phil the bottom of the double-boiler with water and bring it a boil.
*   Pour the raw milk into the top half of the double-boiler. Heat it over the boiling water, stirring thoroughly and consistently throughout the heating process.
*   Use a probe or thermometer to determine when the temperature reaches 165° F. and keep it at 165° F for 15 seconds or more.
*   Set the top half of the double- boiler containing the hot milk in a container of cold water and. Keep the water cold by adding ice as necessary.
*   Continuing to stir slowly and consistently, until the milk is cold, then use immediately or store in the refrigerator.

Microwave method

Raw milk can be pasteurized in a microwave oven by heating the milk to 165°F. Your milk heating temperature should be verified with a probe or thermometer. Stir the milk periodically during the heating period to equalize the temperature. Once 165°F is achieved, the same 15 seconds or more rule must be applied. Throughout. Cool as directed. Pour the hot milk into a pan or dish which is in a container of cold water and keep the water cold by adding ice. Continue to stir until the milk is cold, then use immediately or store in the refrigerator

Sanitizing by Heating/Boiling

Sanitizing and sterilizing the jars and containers in which the milk will be stored to set into yogurt is an important step that is often ignored. If you don't sterilize your containers and lid liners, it can be dangerous as it causes contamination and can weaken your immune system. People simply clean the containers under running water or in dishwashers and just assume that they're good to be used, but that's not really the case. You can easily sanitize your containers and yogurt makers at home before preparation, and we insist on doing so as it's a crucial step to making a safe product that's fit to use and is free of harmful microbes.

Make sure that you give your jars and containers a quick boil to sterilize them. There are also sanitizing options in a few dishwashers. While boiling and heating containers work for sanitization, a few people also prefer using bleach powder for this process. You need to use ¼ teaspoon of bleach for 32 oz of water per quart container. Leave the containers in this solution for about an hour and rinse thoroughly. You can also prepare the solution in advance and store it for future use.

Safe Fermentation Temperature Zone

The fermentation process of turning milk into yogurt takes time—around six to eight hours. But it needs an ideal temperature for the same. The important sugar present in milk, lactose, is necessary for the starter culture bacteria to feed on. These bacteria are the most active at high temperatures. The ideal temperature range for the incubation and fermentation should be between 110°F and 115°F. After you've heated your milk and allowed it to cool, you can add the culture when the temperature has reached 115°F. You can do this by putting the hot milk in a cold double-bath and constantly stirring it. Once it reaches 120°F, take it out of the bath and let the temperature drop by five more degrees.

You can also incubate the milk at around 110°F for six to eight hours to have a smoother texture and more flavor. The texture and taste of the yogurt are determined by the temperature and time it is left to ferment.

How Long to Incubate Yogurt Culture

The incubation process should be given enough time to get yogurt with perfect consistency. As we know by now, bacteria need lactose to feed on to turn the milk into yogurt. Even after setting the yogurt culture for around six to eight hours, you might still find traces of lactose in the milk. It needs more time to set if you need a minimal amount of sugar in your yogurt. This can take around 24 hours in total and can be termed 'sugar-free' or 'lactose-free' yogurt. If you need to follow a specific carbohydrate diet (SCD), you need to incubate the yogurt for up to 30 hours. It's not advisable to ferment it more than that because the bacteria will starve, and it'll ruin the yogurt.

This process of leaving it for 24 hours also helps in eliminating all bad bacteria that might otherwise harm your gut health. Since there is almost no lactose present, the bad bacteria are deprived of lactose, making it healthier for your gut. The specific carbohydrate diet is also apt in this situation and forms a healthier diet option. Also, the longer the yogurt is left to incubate and ferment, the stronger it will taste. For instance, yogurt that's fermented for around 30 hours gets a tart flavor, whereas yogurt that's fermented for only six to eight hours will have a milder taste.

All these stages are crucial to make the perfect yogurt that's flavorful and smooth in texture. Just make a note of the important temperatures and time for each process if you're planning on making yogurt at home. Homogenization, pasteurization, sanitization, and fermentation are the main stages of making yogurt. Pay special attention to the incubation process as it can be quite challenging, especially if you're performing it for the first time. We'll talk about it in further detail while discussing how to make yogurt at home.

Chapter 5: Storing Yogurt

Preparing yogurt takes time, and attention, and so, correctly storing yogurt is important.

How to Store your yogurt

Once your yogurt is done, store your yogurt in the refrigerator. If you have any remaining yogurt from a previous batch, it is strongly recommended that you apply (FIFO). The first-in, first-out (FIFO) technique is a method of rotating your stock so that the oldest is used first, and the newest is use last.

Safe Storage Temperatures

Yogurt stays in the best condition at cool temperatures. You need to keep it refrigerated at all times to prevent the yogurt from spoiling, at a temperature of 34°F to 40°F is required for safe storage. Never make the mistake of storing it at room temperature as it can cause the microorganisms to grow rapidly. The ideal temperature to freeze yogurt is 0°F, and the process lasts longer than usual. Yogurt needs to be kept refrigerated because the microorganisms that are beneficial for your health can die otherwise, and end up causing digestive issues. Every yogurt type functions differently, and so you need to check the label on the container.

How Long Can Yogurt Be Safely Stored?

If you're interested in making yogurt at home, it's only natural you'll want to know how long it will last. Since you won't be adding preservatives as they do in commercial yogurts, you may be worried that it won't last as long. Homemade yogurt lasts for around two weeks with refrigeration. If it goes for a long time, it may go bad. But generally, two weeks is enough to finish two or three liters of yogurt, especially if you have kids who love it. We mentioned earlier that you can use a small amount of your homemade yogurt as a starter for your next batch. It's recommended you use it within 7 days for the best results. However, Your yogurt will remain safe to use for about two weeks.

When storing your yogurt, keep it at the back of your fridge because these are the places where temperatures stay coolest and are the most consistent. Since homemade yogurt is delicate, small temperature changes can negatively affect its longevity. Don't forget to tightly seal the containers carrying your yogurt. Doing that protects it from various odors inside the refrigerator.

How do you if your yogurt has gone bad? If it smells bad, throw it away; it's not safe for consumption. Similarly, if you see it developing mold, dump it. While you may have prepared something sweet, it's not worth taking it, it'll bring you trouble later.

Other Storage Precautions

● Make sure that you aren't cross-contaminating your yogurt. This means that you should always eat it by transferring it to a bowl in small servings instead of eating directly from the container. It's also necessary to use a clean spoon to avoid further contamination. Using a dirty spoon will spoil the yogurt much sooner than its expiry date.

• Check for liquid fluid on top of the yogurt to determine if the yogurt has spoiled. Also, if mold or mild is growing in the yogurt container. If a certain type of yogurt doesn't produce any liquid, you should notice curdling or a puddle formation. Finally, you'll notice mold formation with weird colors and textures as soon as you open the container. This happens when the culture, which once acted as a preservative, dies. This is when yogurt becomes unfit to consume and should be thrown away.

• Don't store your yogurt with a loose lid or a piece of aluminum foil. Keep it away from external air.

Follow these storage and temperature precautions to keep your yogurt fit for consumption until the expiry date. As we've mentioned before, yogurt takes a lot of resources and time to form, and so it requires the utmost care when it comes to storage.

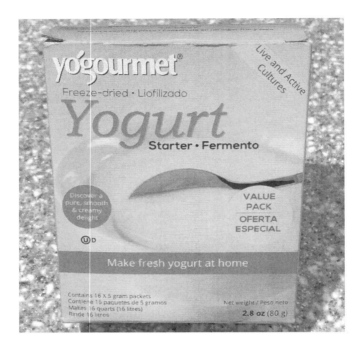

Chapter 6: Sources of Yogurt Culture

The yogurt culture is the most crucial ingredient in making yogurt because it is entirely responsible for the end product. As we know by now, yogurt culture is a group of helpful bacteria that convert the treated milk into yogurt. So, it's important to choose an appropriate culture that suits your needs and produces the best results. Among the many brands and yogurt culture types that are available today, it can get confusing to choose one and store it for further use.

This chapter will cover the different aspects of yogurt culture, including commercial and live culture sources to give your yogurt a silky texture with a great taste, along with ways to preserve and maintain the culture.

Types of Yogurt Culture

To know more about storing yogurt culture, we should first take a look at the various types that are available to understand your needs and choose one accordingly.

Direct-Set Cultures

Also known as single-use cultures, these are used to make only one batch of yogurt, as the name suggests. To use this type of culture for more than one time, you can use the cultured yogurt in the new batch of prepared milk. But don't overuse it, as it will not fetch the ideal results after a few batches.

Heirloom Cultures

Also known as reusable cultures, these are used to prepare an indefinite number of batches. However, these need to be used at least once every seven days to keep the bacteria active. You can prepare new batches through old yogurt portions made from an heirloom culture.

Mesophilic Cultures

This type of culture works best at room temperature. The milk takes relatively longer (around 12 to 18 hours) to ferment, as the culture is added to cold milk that doesn't require preheating. The resultant yogurt is, however, not quite dense.

Thermophilic Cultures

Contrary to mesophilic culture, this type functions the best at higher temperatures. Add it to the heated milk and let it ferment for around 5 to 12 hours. The resultant yogurt is quite dense and thick. This type of culture requires a hot source at all times to function properly.

Live-Culture, Store-Bought Yogurt

This is probably the least inexpensive way to buy culture to produce yogurt. Among the numerous brands and variety of yogurts that are available at any grocery store, you need to choose one that states, "contains live/active/probiotic cultures." This kind of yogurt is the most suitable to form new batches at home, as it carries live cultures. The most common type of yogurt that promotes live culture is made from cow's milk. You can, however, also choose soymilk yogurt, goat milk yogurt, and sheep milk yogurt. In case you don't find a live-culture yogurt, you can simply purchase normal cow's milk yogurt to prepare a new batch.

Popular Commercial Sources

Popular commercial sources for yogurt culture include countertop yogurt starters and freeze-dried yogurt cultures. The former is basically a type of mesophilic culture and functions in a temperature range of 70°F to 74°F. These are quite easy to use, as well. This kind comes in a variety of yogurt types—Greek, Finnish, Bulgarian, and Georgian—giving you a chance to try out different types of yogurt.

The other type, the freeze-dried starter culture, comes in a powder form and is preferred by vegans as it is dairy-free. These can, however, be a lot more expensive than normal cultures. You can also find a lot of useful bacteria in this type, which makes it more beneficial.

How to Preserve, Propagate, and Maintain Your Yogurt Culture

At times, you might buy your culture pack in larger quantities, decide to use it for more than one or two times, or want to save it for later use. In this case, it's important to preserve, propagate, and maintain your yogurt culture for maximum effectiveness and desired results. You can do this by refrigerating, freezing, or drying the culture packs.

Refrigeration and Freezing

Freezing is an ideal option when you want to use the starter culture for up to four weeks of the purchase date. Here's how you can do it: take a freezer-safe container or an ice cube tray and put the active culture in it. Around one tablespoon of yogurt is required to ferment one cup of milk. Add the culture to every section of the ice cube tray, depending on the dimensions of the tray. Freeze these until they are solid and put them in an airtight container for storage. Once that is done, you can thaw them in the refrigerator for further use. Leaving them at room temperature for thawing can destroy the culture, and so it's advisable to thaw them in the refrigerator.

This might take some time, but it'll save your yogurt from damage. Once the culture is thawed, you can use this cube for preparing yogurt by simply adding it to the prepared milk. Make sure that you don't freeze the culture cubes for a longer time as it can diminish the activity of these microorganisms. And if it has been frozen for a month or more, use more than one culture cube to incubate your mixture.

Storage Duration

If you want to store the culture for up to three months of the purchase date, you need to dry it out for safer use. To do this, take a piece of unbleached parchment paper and spread about two tablespoons of starter culture on it. Find a moisture-free space that stays under 80°F for the starter culture to dry. Once it dries out completely, put the dried matter in a Zip-lock bag, and store it in the refrigerator. You can use this dried culture safely for up to three months. To use the dry culture, you can read the instructions on the brand's label, as every brand differs in directions and the ideal conditions to prepare yogurt.

Apart from yogurt culture, you'd need to learn more about the other equipment and tools required to make yogurt. Read on to find out about those in the next chapter.

Chapter 7: Yogurt Making Equipment and Supplies

Yogurt-making is simpler than cooking; you need only assemble the equipment and ingredients, then let them do the hard work.

Milk or Milk Substitute

In an earlier chapter discussed the various milk types and milk substitutes for making yogurt. Perhaps, the most common milk used to make yogurt at home is cow's milk. Whole cow's milk is rich in fat and produces yogurt that has great texture and flavor.

People who have weight or health concerns may switch to 1% and 2% milk or even skim milk to make yogurt. 1% and 2% milk and skim milk contain lower fat while providing tasty nutrition.

For folks who have access to milk from other animals' milk, such as goat's milk, can prepare yogurts with differing texture and tastes.

Vegetarians or people who wish to avoid dairy can use milk alternatives like soymilk, rice milk, or almond milk to make dairy-free yogurt.

A Saucepan

A nonstick or stainless-steel saucepan is a piece of important equipment for making yogurt, when working with raw milk or if you plan to heat your milk during the yogurt making process. A deep saucepan made of thick metal usually works best.

Yogurt Culture

Choosing the right yogurt culture for you is important. Yogurt culture can have a major impact on the thickness, texture, and flavor of your yogurt in addition to the other components. Choosing the correct yogurt culture for you may require some experimentation. While it is possible to start making yogurt from plain commercial yogurt with live culture, you may be more satisfied over time by choosing a yogurt starter culture which made more closely align with your personal tastes preferences.

Saving yogurt culture

you can save your yogurt culture refrigerated in a sealed container. To do this, you should always save the culture from the most recent successful batch of yogurt. I would recommend that you don't keep this culture in the refrigerator for more than two or three weeks before making a new culture to revitalize it and to keep it from spoiling in the refrigerator. And a new sample should be kept from each successive successful batch to ensure the vigor and freshness of your yogurt culture.

Yogurt Incubation

there are several methods of incubating your yogurt, some of which are described below. However, from a consistency and ease of use point of view, I have found that using an electric yogurt incubator works best for me.

Electronic Yogurt Maker/Incubator

electric yogurt makers and incubators can be simple or complex depending on your needs and the way you work in the kitchen. I tend to prefer the simplistic versions of basically an on-off switch, but there are other characteristics that people find important, which may include the following.

• The Capacity Of The Yogurt Maker

the capacity of your chosen yogurt maker or incubator is important because you needed to make sufficient yogurt for the number of persons in your household, which will regularly consume yogurt and the rate at which your family uses the yogurt. Keeping in mind the number of ways in which your family may be using yogurt in cooking, in drinks like smoothies, or just eating the yogurt in a dish or a bowl. Also, a large capacity yogurt maker may actually keep you from making more yogurt because your refrigerator is overstocked and may even lead to spoilage.

A Built-In Timer

• A built-in timer and shut off switch for some may be useful if there are concerns about becoming distracted and not knowing when to check your yogurt for doneness, depending on the style of yogurt you intend to make. I will admit that I never bothered with a timer I generally start my yogurt at times that the rhythms of my life will bring me back to within sight of my yogurt incubator at a time when the yogurt should approximately be done. Additionally, I tend to leave my make yogurt maker in plain sight on my kitchen counter so that it won't be forgotten in some dark corner of my kitchen or pantry when I'm making yogurt.

• A Built-In Cooling System

Some yogurt makers or incubators Cooling systems to rapidly cool the yogurt and stop the fermentation process. This cooling system may be useful if you're making yogurt in an unintended manner while at work or away for a while. I don't usually bother with this feature. I tend to move my yogurt directly from the incubator to the refrigerator when it is ready. I find it moving directly in the refrigerator when it is ready, allows the yogurt to cool rapidly, and stores the yogurt until ready for use.

● Price Point

the price point of an electric yogurt incubator or maker is important. Not only does it need to fit within your budget, but if you're not a regular yogurt maker today, how much are you willing to spend on a machine that you may tire of and stop using later. Consider what you really need from a yogurt maker or incubator and go for the lowest-cost, highest quality, value .4 your purchase. Buying a yogurt maker should not be a vanity statement or a fashion statement or a kitchen architecture statement. Electric yogurt makers and or incubators are kitchen appliances like any other and should be treated as such

Low-Temperature Oven

the low-temperature oven method is a classic alternative to an electric yogurt maker or incubator. For gas oven's the pilot light usually provides enough heat for this method ever electric ovens turning on the oven light can serve the same purpose. However, you will need to make sure that these do, in fact, keep the oven warm enough to allow your yogurt culture to grow efficiently. Placing an oven thermometer and a canning jar of water will allow you to quickly see the temperature of the oven without having to open the oven door and allowing heat to escape. I'm not really a fan of this method, but if you're in a tight spot or just making the occasional batch of yogurt, the low-temperature oven method is an idea worth considering.

Electric Blanket

Using an electric blanket with an adjustable thermostat can be an effective method for making yogurt. Key elements of this method will be verified that the temperature is, in fact, staying within the appropriate temperature range. Also, that you have an out-of-the-way, safe place to put the electric blanket and yogurt while it ferments away from the hazards of running kid's family pets in the Yard mishap. The electric blanket method, once you prepare your milk and add your yogurt culture, it really is just a matter of wrapping up your yogurt fermentation containers and in a preheated electric blanket with an appropriately set thermostat setting. Then, leave your yogurt culture to ferment for the required time according to the type of yogurt you're making. Try not to unwrap and check the yogurt, if possible. This will allow the electric blanket to maintain the appropriate temperature more easily.

Heating Pad

the heating pad method is conceptually summer to the electric blanket method, except you're using a heating pad as the heat source. To prepare your heating pad incubator, you'll want a towel or small blanket, an electric heating pad, and a safe place to protect your jars once covered. Set the heating pad set to an appropriate setting, which you may want to test with a thermometer and a canning jar of water. Then, wrap or cover the prepared jars with towels or a small blanket and let sit for the desired fermentation.

Slow Cooker/Crockpot

slow cooker/crockpot method is another alternative to make yogurt. Making yogurt in your slow cooker also was a way to get more value on that kitchen appliance if you find that you don't frequently use it. However, not all yogurt cultures are suitable for making yogurt in a slow cooker, and you'll definitely need to do your research and choose a starter culture that is compatible with the slow cooker method and meet your flavor and texture desires.

Insulated Cooler with Hot Water Bottles

The insulated cooler with bottles of hot water approach is a time-tested method. To use the insulated cooler with bottles of hot water method, the basic steps are:

- Prepare a clean and sanitized insulated cooler with a tight-fitting lid.
- Prepare yogurt milk to be fermented in Sealed canning jars at 110^0F.
- A towel for wrapping the yogurt jars.
- Place yogurt jars in the towel-lined insulated cooler with sealed jars of hot water.
- Cover all jars with another towel and close the lid of the cooler.
- Let the yogurt ferment for the required hours according to the style of yogurt being made.
- Remove yogurt from the cooler and place it in the refrigerator immediately to chill.

Towel-Wrapped Thermos

The towel wrapped Thermos method can also be used to make yogurt at home. To use The towel wrapped Thermos method:

- Preheat the thermos with hot 110^{0}F water.
- Then, quickly empty the thermos and refill with your warmed yogurt milk for fermentation
- And firmly seal your thermos fill with yogurt milk
- wrap in a dense tower small blanket to help keep it warm
- Let the yogurt ferment for the required hours according to the style of yogurt being made.
- Remove yogurt from the thermos and place it in the refrigerator immediately to chill.

Yogurt Storage Cups/Jars

storage container for your yogurt is important. While you can store yogurt in any container, you choose as long as it is sealable. Serving size containers work best so that members of the family can grab and go or if using a recipe, you can typically be measured based on how many containers you grabbed. 6 to 8-ounce containers are usually best for storing yogurt. Widemouth containers or jars are strongly recommended as it will facilitate the removal of the yogurt either for consumption or for reuse in recipes. I'll be honest here, I usually leave my yogurt in the incubator jars which are 6-ounce glass jars, but not Widemouth and I have enough jars to make at least two batches if I so desire. Regardless of the size of storage containers, you use the first–in-out method (FIFO) should be used, whereby the oldest yogurt is moved forward in the refrigerator for immediate consumption and the newest batch is placed behind all existing yogurt containers.

Chapter 8: Tips for Making Yogurt

Making yogurt at home is pretty easy, but it may still seem intimidating to a few people. Even though the preparation is simple and just takes a few steps, the process is lengthy and takes around one day to yield results. But it's healthier and cheaper, so regular consumers prefer to make it at home. If you've decided to do it too, it's time for you to learn some hacks and methods to do it correctly and achieve exceptional results.

For this, we need to discuss a few additional tips concerning yogurt-making, including the recommended practices and the things to avoid. With these tips, making yogurt at home should become easier.

Recommended Practices

Allow the Yogurt Culture to Grow Before Incubation

Typically, I whisk in my yogurt culture starter into my room temperature milk base in a large bowl, and then I cover the bowl and let the mixture stand for 20 to 30 minutes allowing the culture activating grow. Then, I give it a good stir before placing the cultured milk into the incubator bottles. This helps to ensure that all incubator bottles have a healthy dose fo the culture for more even fermentation.

Making Plain Yogurt before Adding Flavoring and Sweeteners

You may make a mistake of adding flavorings and sweeteners in the middle of the process, even before the yogurt is set. Avoid adding sugar and sweeteners before fermentation. You need to add the ingredients only after the yogurt is set and chilled. To sweeten it, we'd recommend using natural ingredients such as maple syrup or honey—we'll discuss this recipe in detail in the last chapter—or jam to give it a fruity flavor. You can also add specific flavor extracts per cup of yogurt according to your preferences. Add a flavor or sweetener that doesn't cause lumps and can blend well with the yogurt to gain an even texture.

Straining the Yogurt

Straining the yogurt makes it thicker, which is often done while making Greek-style yogurt. It also helps in eliminating the additional lumps that could damage the silky-smooth texture of the yogurt. With this process, you can separate the whey from the yogurt, which can then be used to drink separately or as a cooking ingredient. You'll need a mesh cheesecloth for this process. Set a bowl underneath the cheesecloth and pour your yogurt into the cloth. Use a spoon or ladle to force the yogurt through it. This will strain the entire mixture, and you'll be left with thick and flavorful yogurt. If you choose to strain your yogurt, avoid using powdered milk as it doesn't help in making thicker yogurt.

How To Check If The Yogurt Is Done

After the first 5 hours, it is okay to start checking hourly if your yogurt is done. When ready, your yogurt should start looking firm, according to the texture of the type of yogurt you are making. Moreover, it will get more acidic with each passing hour.

To be honest, when making traditional yogurt, I typically try to time my yogurt making so that I started three or four hours before I go to bed at night, and check the fermenting yogurt first thing in the morning. This usually gives it about eight hours and results in a consistent Lee ready batch of yogurt to be moved into the refrigerator.

What If the Milk Doesn't Change to Yogurt?

There are two reasons why your milk may not turn into yogurt. One, you may have allowed the milk to get too cold after heating. Cool temperatures cannot support effective fermentation. Always ensure the temperatures are maintained at 110-115ºF throughout the incubation period. Second, you may have used a weak starter. If you're buying plain yogurt to use as your starter, make sure it's as fresh as possible. The fresher it is, the more active the cultures, and the better the results.

Choose a Good Culture

Live culture, popularly known as the yogurt starter culture, is bacteria that help to ferment the milk. There are plenty of yogurt starter options to choose from. While all yogurt starter cultures do the same thing on milk, there is some nuance of using different cultures. It is, therefore, important to consider which type of culture is ideal for your lifestyle. Most starter cultures are direct-set or single-use, meaning they can only make one batch of yogurt.

Other yogurt starters are heirloom or reusable, meaning they can be used several times by adding a bit of yogurt from the previous batch to a new batch and so on. If you are using non-dairy milk to make yogurt, you will have to use a vegan starter culture.

Choose A Good Container For Your Yogurt

The preferable vessels are the ones that will help in retaining heat during rest. You don't have to go buying expensive specialized gallons for your yogurt. Large ceramic bowls or crocks will do the job. Cover the containers with small pot lids or pans. Avoid using metallic vessels because they won't retain heat, and the yogurt won't set up correctly. The yogurt won't set up if the conditions are too cold.

Use The Right Temperatures

There are three stages of preparing yogurt; boiling the milk, adding live culture and incubation. To get the best yogurt, ensure the milk is at the ideal temperature at all the stages. The guidelines below will help you:

- When you boil the milk, ensure that it comes to a full boil so that all bacteria are killed. Any other bacteria that are not the live culture will lower the quality of your yogurt.

- Add the culture at the right temperatures. If you add the culture while the milk is too hot, all the starter bacteria will be killed, and if you add it cold, the live culture bacteria will not activate. The correct temperature to add culture is when the milk is warm.

- When incubating the yogurt, the milk needs to be warm. Cold temperatures will deactivate the live culture. This is why you should use a bowl that retains heat for the longest time possible. You can put some cloth down the covered bowl to help insulate it.

How To Thicken Yogurt

How to thicken yogurt?

Several factors can affect the thickness and quality of your yogurt. So, here are a few pointers to help you make a thicker yogurt if that's what you're looking for. Multiple approaches can be used in combination to help make a thick and tasty yogurt, some traditional and some not so traditional.

Why thicken yogurt

There are many good reasons to thicken your yogurt, which can range from the simple texture of the yogurt when eaten by the intended future use of the yogurt when you make it. Some people like a nice thick spoonful of yogurt was some fruit in it for breakfast or snack, and in other cases, people are going to use yogurt to make smoothies, icebox pies, cheesecakes, and other recipes which require a thick yogurt, Greek yogurt, or yogurt cheese.

Another good reason to make thick yogurts is nutritional density, the thicker your yogurt, the more overall nutrition you get, and every spoonful. There's nothing wrong with having a nice tasty yogurt drink, but a nice thick bite of yogurt cheesecake will have more nutrition per spoonful.

Cooking is a very common reason to want a thicker yogurt; many recipes in modern times actually request things like Greek yogurt is ingredients. The straining process used in making Greek yogurt is only one of several options for thickening your yogurt. It is possible to have a yogurt every bit as thick as Greek yogurt and never go through the straining process.

When to start thinking about your yogurt thickening process

The best time to start thinking about your yogurt thickening process is when preparing to make your yogurt. Many factors go into how thick your yogurt will be and careful consideration, and planning will facilitate the process.

Choose the best dairy products ingredients

The ingredients that you use have a very major impact on how thick your yogurt will be. Using whole milk rather than 1% or 2% milk will add a significant amount of milk solids and fats to thicken your yogurt. Besides, adding other elements to the milk, you've chosen for making yogurt such as a proportion of cream, half-and-half, Media Crema (table cream), or unreconstituted powdered milk can significantly thicken the final result. I have experimented with these combinations and find that any of them or a combination of them works just fine. The pointers I would provide are:

- first, and perhaps most importantly, I will recommend that you start slow and add a little bit of whatever thickeners you intend to incorporate in increasing quantities until you reach the appearance, texture, and flavor outcome you desire. Some of the thickening additives will not only change the thickness but will also affect the texture, taste, and appearance of your yogurt. Finding that balance for your family loves your yogurt is important.

- Secondly, every batch of yogurt need not be made the same. If you're planning to use the yogurt for everyday use as a snack, then a whole milk yogurt may be thick enough and make everyone happy. However, if you're planning to make your yogurt as a replacement for cream cheese, you may want to make a thicker batch for the specific use and further strain the yogurt to achieve the desired density.
- If you're going to add unreconstituted powdered milk, I would recommend that you start with one package and work your way up. Also, try to buy powdered milk with the fewest possible ingredients. Powdered milk with too many preservatives and salts added to them can actually kill your yogurt culture if added high enough proportions.
- When adding unreconstituted powdered milk, I have gone as far as adding two, 3.2 ounce (90.7 G) envelopes with satisfactory results.
- As you start on your yogurt thickening journey, I would recommend that you start the more common kinds of milk and creams. Then, work your way into the more commercial and preservative forms, if you feel you want to. I suggested hierarchy for working your way into using yogurt thickeners would be:

1. using whole milk
2. adding half-and-half
3. adding heavy cream or whipping cream
4. adding evaporated milk
5. adding unreconstituted powdered milk

Choose your yogurt culture

The yogurt culture you choose to use will have a significant impact on how thick your final product will be, perhaps, more so than in the additive you may add to the yogurt later. So I would recommend that you experiment with different yogurt cultures until you find one that has the texture and flavor characteristics your family likes. There are several sites online where a variety of yogurt cultures can be purchased. Ordering a few different small samples to experiment with can be a very rewarding experience.

When Heating your milk

if you're working with raw milk or you choose to heat your milk before making yogurt, then lengthening you're heating time may help thicken your yogurt. Linking your heating time is a traditional method described in different cookbooks. However, I will admit I don't actually use this process. But if you want to try it yourself, go about it. If you heat the milk a little longer, it will denature the protein molecules and will result in better attachment when they come in contact with lactic acid. Make sure that the milk stays at 180°F constantly for around 20 to 30 minutes while you're heating it. This will result in yogurt that's thick, creamy, and firm. Also, make sure that you're heating the milk slowly and not speeding up the process to avoid a grainy texture.

During the fermentation process

During the fermentation process and depending on the type of yogurt you're making, you can extend the fermentation a few hours, which will allow the yogurt culture to work on the lactose and thicken your yogurt a little more. However, extending your fermentation duration definitely has a point of diminishing return in which the thickening yogurt becomes more bitter as a result of the fermentation process, so start by extending your fermentation by an hour or two at a time and see how it turns out.

After you have fermented your yogurt

Once your yogurt has finished its fermentation process, then, the more traditional thickening method of storing your yogurt can be applied. This is a very common approach when making Greek yogurt or yogurt cheese. The real difference here is in the duration of straining that is applied. Greek yogurt is strained less than yogurt cheese and therefore is less dense. How thick your yogurt was before you started straining it combined with how long you strain your yogurt dictate the density of your final yogurt. Also, yogurt can only be strained so much, at some point, there will be no more meaningful liquid to strain out.

If you're planning to strain your yogurt, for best results, I recommend moving your yogurt into the straining process immediately upon removal from the fermentation process. This will allow the yogurt to softer and more flexible and will allow more liquid to escape more rapidly early in the straining process. However, refrigerated yogurt can also be strained to achieve similar results.

How Long to strain yogurt

Truthfully, how long storing yogurt depends on the results you want. If you're looking for slightly thicker yogurt, then three or four hours of straining might be plenty. However, if you're looking for Greek yogurt, then you want to strain your yogurt overnight approximately 10-12 hours or perhaps more. If you desire to make a thicker Greek yogurt or yogurt cheese, then continue to strain, and you want to check the consistency about every six hours or until liquid ceases to strain out. Once you reach the consistency desired, remove the thickened yogurt or yogurt cheese from the strainer and move it into the desired storage containers or using it immediately.

Things to Avoid

Here are a few pointers to avoid unwanted results, and to make your yogurt is nutritious and flavorful as you like it to be.

Avoid Adding Nondairy Ingredients as Much as Possible

For a perfect and authentic batch of yogurt, it's better to avoid additional non-dairy ingredients, especially artificial ones such as processed sweeteners or flavorings. The yogurt should be as unadulterated as possible. A lot of people use additional ingredients such as jam, flavoring, fruit, etc. As long as you don't need flavored yogurt, we'd recommend not using an additional ingredient as it can ruin the yogurt's shelf life and freshness.

Many people also use gelatin to thicken their yogurt. While it provides exceptional results in terms of thickness and texture, we don't recommend using it because it can ruin the flavor. Use other methods to thicken your yogurt, as discussed above, instead of using artificial ingredients. It is possible to use gelatin for quicker results, along with other thickeners such as pectin, milk solids, agar, guar gum, and arrowroot starch, but we'd still suggest you avoid these.

Don't Culture the Yogurt for Too Long

Time and temperature are two important factors to which you need to pay maximum attention while preparing yogurt. Take a note of the temperature when you add the culture to the milk, and don't let it rise above the recommended mark for a long time. This will ruin the taste and texture of the resultant yogurt; you'll end up having yogurt that's sour in taste and lumpy in texture. If you're using a thermophilic yogurt culture, you need to make sure that the temperature is set in between 108°F and 112°F.

Also, always try to use a fresh starter that's not older than a week. As we've mentioned before, starter cultures in powdered form tend to work best. Culture your yogurt for around 8 to 12 hours, 24 hours being the maximum. If you don't want your yogurt to be sour, you can also culture it at a lower temperature until you get your desired taste.

While you're at it, make sure you use clean equipment to make your yogurt, as this can prevent contamination and mold formation. So, clean equipment and fresh ingredients are a must. By following these simple tips, you no longer have to feel intimidated by the process. We're sure that you'll fetch remarkable results by keeping these in mind.

Chapter 9: How to Make Yogurt at Home

We've now arrived at the most important part, making the yogurt. This chapter is all about making traditional yogurt with different types of milk that we mentioned in the earlier chapters, along with other kinds of yogurt such as Greek, Australian, Viili, Kefir, Ayran, Yakult, and Icelandic Skyr.

How to make yogurt from pasteurized milk

Since store-bought milk in the United States is pasteurized, this will be the most frequently used method for making the traditional yogurt found in the American marketplace.

What You Need:

- **Milk** – You can make yogurt from whole milk, 2% skimmed milk, organic and local milk. However, whole pasteurized milk is usually the most commonly used as a foundation for making yogurt.
- **Starter culture** – The options available for your starter culture include powdered starter culture, store-bought yogurt, or homemade yogurt from a previous batch.
- **Yogurt Incubator** – The incubator is essential for maintaining your milk and culture mix at about 110 F to 115 F for close to five hours. Therefore, options available to you include a yogurt maker, thermos, or heat keeper jugs. You can also use several mason jars filled with hot water and placed in a cooler.
- **Other requirements** – A large spoon or whisk, storage containers, ladle, mixing bowl.

Directions:

- **Clean all your tools**

It is always advisable to wash and even sterilize all your yogurt, making equipment and surfaces to avoid introducing other unwanted bacteria. Some clean their tools with boiling water, but thorough handwashing is also enough.

- **Start with room temperature milk**

If you're starting with refrigerated milk, you will want to warm the milk to room temperature before adding your yogurt starter culture. This, for me, generally is not a problem, since I tend to use pasteurized box milk from my pantry shelves.

- **Add your starter culture**

When using a yogurt powdered starter, it is okay to whisk it in according to the amount specified on the package instructions.

- **yogurt as a starter culture**

However, when using yogurt as a starter culture, it is advisable to first isolate a small amount of the milk and keep adding it to the starter culture and stir until all of it has been mixed. This is because adding cold yogurt directly to the milk will slow down the incubation by suddenly dropping the temperatures too much.

- **Incubate**

Use your spoon or ladle to transfer the milk and culture mix to your incubator of choice. The primary importance of incubation is to maintain your milk and culture mix at the stated temperature for 5 to 10 hours undisturbed. However, keep in mind that shorter incubation periods under cooler temperatures will produce sweeter, thinner yogurt while longer and hotter incubation periods will produce tarter and thicker yogurt.

- **Checking yogurt for doneness**

When ready, your yogurt should start looking firm. Moreover, it will get more acidic with each passing hour.

- **Store your yogurt**

Once your yogurt is done, store your yogurt in the refrigerator

How to Make Yogurt From Unpasteurized (Raw) Milk

Making yogurt with unpasteurized raw milk is pretty much the same as making it from pasteurized milk you might bite the store. However, there are a couple of essential points to consider for your own health and safety:

- first, you need to be sure that you get your fresh raw milk from a reputable source that you trust.
- Second, you need to be sure the milk comes from healthy animals that are not taking antibiotics are being treated for some form of disease or illness.
- Lastly, unpasteurized raw milk must be brought to the boiling point (at Least 180°F / 82°C) and pasteurized before making yogurt from it. Otherwise, any number of unhealthy bacteria can be in that milk, including such nasty critters as E. coli.

I grew up on a home farm where my mother always kept small stable milk cows, and we drank our milk raw. It certainly didn't do anything to us except keep us healthy. Still, my mother and all of us were exceptionally careful about the milking process, collection, and immediate refrigeration of our milk. If there was doubt about the safety of the milk, it was thrown out. My mother put much emphasis on the "when in doubt throw it out" rule, which still I live by today regarding all food.

Admittedly, most American cooks will not have an opportunity to work with raw milk.

However, if someone who may have the opportunity, here are the instructions.

What You Need:

- **Milk** – You can make yogurt from whole milk or skimmed (cream removed) fresh raw milk.
- **Starter culture** – The options available for your starter culture include powdered starter culture, store-bought yogurt, or homemade yogurt from a previous batch.
- **Yogurt Incubator** – The incubator is important for maintaining your milk and culture mix at about 110 F to 115 F for close to five to eight hours. Therefore, options available to you include a yogurt maker, thermos, or heat keeper jugs. You maintain the needed temperatures for the required amount of time, and you ensure equal distribution of heat throughout the incubator to prevent the occurrence of some hot and cool spots.
- **Other requirements** – include heavy, large pots, candy thermometer (preferably one with a clip for attachment), large spoon or whisk, storage containers, cheesecloth,

colander, ladle, both large and small bowls.

Directions

- **Clean all your tools**

Did you know that you actually need a bacterium known as *Lactobacillus bulgaricus* to make good yogurt? Given all the microorganisms, including other bacteria present all around us, it is always advisable to wash and even sterilize all your yogurt making equipment and surfaces to avoid introducing other unwanted bacteria. Some clean their tools with boiling water, but thorough handwashing is also enough.

- **Heat the milk**

--- Important --

Unpasteurized (raw) milk must be heated to near to the boiling point, not boiled, to kill the bacteria.

Additionally, heating the milk for some extra minutes helps in concentrating it so that your yogurt can be thicker.

- **Cool the milk**

After heating your milk to the boiling point, cool it back down to 110 F-115 F. Make use of your thermometer to track the temperatures. Also, keep stirring to ensure even cooling.

- **Add your starter culture**

When using a yogurt powdered starter, it is okay to whisk it in according to the amount specified on the package instructions.

However, when using yogurt as a starter culture, it is advisable to first isolate a small amount of the milk and keep adding it to the starter culture and stir until all of it has been mixed. This is because adding cold yogurt directly to the milk will slow down the incubation by suddenly dropping the temperatures too much.

- **Incubate**

Use your spoon or ladle to transfer the milk and culture mix to your incubator of choice. The primary importance of incubation is to maintain your milk and culture mix at the stated temperature for 5 to 10 hours undisturbed. However, keep in mind that shorter incubation periods under cooler temperatures will produce sweeter, thinner yogurt while longer and hotter incubation periods will produce tarter and thicker yogurt.

- **Checking yogurt for doneness**

When ready, your yogurt should start looking firm. Moreover, it will get more acidic with each passing hour.

- **Store your yogurt**

- Once your yogurt is done, store your yogurt in the refrigerator

How To Make Yogurt From Different Kinds Of Commercial Milks

We may not always have whole milk available with which to make yogurt, or we may for personal or health reasons may need to use an alternative to whole milk. Or we may simply want to experiment with other types of milk. So, here are some quick guidelines for making yogurt with the more common commercial milk alternatives.

How to Make Traditional Yogurt with Half-and-Half

Making traditional yogurt with Half-and-Half requires no special treatment and can be made following the procedure for making yogurt with pasteurized milk. However, if you use Half-and-Half straight, the yogurt will be very thick along the lines of Greek yogurt. If you like a lighter yogurt, then you will want to dilute the Half-and-Half. To dilute Half-and-Half to a whole milk equivalent, use a 1 to 4 ratio (1 cup Half-and-Half with 4 cups filtered water added).

How to Make Traditional Yogurt with 1 %, 2%, or Skimmed Milk

1 %, 2%, or Skimmed milk are alternatives to whole milk and can be made following the procedure for making yogurt with pasteurized

milk. However, the yogurt made with 1 % or 2% milk will produce a yogurt with fewer milk solids and non-yogurt liquid once fermentation is completed. So, you will want to quickly drain off the excess liquid (the method used for Greek yogurt) using an abbreviate straining period.

How to Make Yogurt with Evaporated or Condensed (Unsweetened) Milk

Making traditional yogurt with Evaporated Or condensed (unsweetened) milk requires no special treatment and can be made following the procedure for making yogurt with pasteurized milk. However, if you use condensed (unsweetened) straight, the yogurt will be very thick along the lines of Greek yogurt. If you like a lighter yogurt, then you will want to dilute the condensed (unsweetened). To dilute condensed (unsweetened) to a whole milk equivalent, use a 1 to 1 ratio (1 cup Evaporated milk with 1 cup filtered water added). Please note that unsweetened condensed milk is very uncommon in the United States, so, if you are dealing with condensed milk, please verify that you are, in fact, working with unsweetened condensed before attempting these instructions.

How to Make Yogurt with Sweetened Condensed Milk

Personally, I do not recommend making yogurt with undiluted sweetened condensed milk. For much the same reason that sweetened condensed milk is not considered an alternative to whole milk (even if diluted). The excess sugar in sweetened condensed milk will make the yogurt culture more active than usual (even if diluted). Sweetened condensed milk will result in a more bitter yogurt upon completion of the fermentation process.

To make yogurt with sweetened condensed milk, dilute the sweetened condensed milk with a ratio of 1 to 16 with whole milk (about ½ cup of sweetened condensed milk with 8 cups whole milk); Then, follow the procedure for making yogurt with pasteurized milk.

How to Make Yogurt with Lactose-Free Milk

Making yogurt with Lactose-Free Milk, simply, follow the procedure for making yogurt with pasteurized milk with one exception. When making yogurt with Lactose-Free Milk, follow the process for making yogurt with pasteurized milk with one exception. When making yogurt with Lactose-Free Milk, you will need to extend the incubation period to 18 - 20 hours.

How to Make Yogurt with Powdered Milk

Even though powdered milk isn't a preferred choice among many yogurt makers, it's still an option. You can use it, especially if there aren't other options available to you, or if you just want to experiment.

One reason why some people do not prefer powdered milk is that it's very thin; it doesn't produce as much thickness as you would get when using other types of milk, such as whole milk or half-and-half. It also doesn't taste that great, but that taste diminishes when the milk is converted into yogurt.

To make yogurt powdered milk, reconstitute the powdered milk according to the packaging instructions. Then, follow the procedure for making yogurt with pasteurized milk. A couple of pointers here, not all powdered milk is the same, try to choose powdered milk with the least amount of salts and preservatives, these can affect the flavor of the yogurt and in high enough concentrations kill the yogurt culture—been there and done that. Also, if you have another milk available, which you can add to the powdered milk, like some whole milk, evaporated milk, or half-and-half, or even a little unsweetened cream, these can improve the constancy and flavor of yogurt made from powdered milk.

How to Make Greek Yogurt at Home

Making greek yogurt is not as hard as it seems. And once you can produce it at a consistency that you really like, you can add just about anything to it. Put some honey, maybe nuts, and any kind of sweet berry that will complement its rich, sweet, sour, and cheesy taste. It is perfect for a great snack, or even as a finishing dessert.

What is Greek Yogurt?

For one, plain yogurt is food made through the process of fermentation of milk. The fermentation itself is done with yogurt cultures.

Greek yogurt is regular yogurt, except that after the whole process of making it, there is an additional step.

The finished product is strained well before finally being served. Greek Yogurt is a much thicker version of the plain yogurt that the Greeks traditionally make. It is thick, creamier, more flavorful, and densely packed.

How to Make Greek Yogurt or Strained Yogurt

Equipment

- ·Strainer or Colander
- ·Cheesecloth or muslin
- ·Thin dish towel
- ·Medium to large-sized bowl
- ·Piece of string

Cook's Note

- Honestly, for the cheesecloth, I use a clean piece of an old white t-shirt, and it works just fine.

Ingredients:

- 2 to 3 cups (or more) of plain (unsweetened, unflavored) yogurt

Directions

- Place the colander over the bowl.
- Cut the cheesecloth into manageable sizes, preferably at 17-inch rectangular shapes
- Line colander with cheesecloth squares of up to 8 layers or less.
- Pour the yogurt right into the middle of the cheesecloth.
- With the yogurt inside, tie up the cheesecloth into a bundle using the kitchen twine. Avoid pressing the bundle. Just go ahead and let it rest and allow the cloth to do the work.
- Excess liquid will be naturally squeezed from the bundle into the bowl.
- You can also use muslin or some other similar filter in place of the cheesecloth.

- Place the bowl with the colander and the yogurt bundle inside the refrigerator. Allow the liquid to strain into the bowl right through the colander. Check after an hour. The liquid should not be white. It can be milky, but it should not be chunky
- If you see some white chunks of white stuff in it, it could be that your cheesecloth isn't thick enough. You are probably losing more yogurt than liquid. Add a few more layers of cheesecloth as needed, and once liquid becomes clear, it should be good.
- The more time you take to strain the yogurt, the thicker it will be. To attain Greek yogurt consistency, strain it from 12-48 hours. You can check every 12 hours just in case you already reach the consistency that you want. Also, you may want to dispose of drained off liquid, when you check your yogurt. Then, you can remove the Greek Yogurt from the strainer.
- If you would like to reach the consistency of thick labneh cheese, allow it to sit and strain from 48-72

hours. After that, you can add salt to taste. You can also adjust the amount as desired.

- After straining, remove from the bowl and serve or place in a sealed container and refrigerate until use.

Storing Greek Yogurt

Once your yogurt is done, store your yogurt in the refrigerator

How To Make Instant Pot Australian (Noosa) Yogurt At Home

If you've never tasted the Australian Noosa yogurt, then you don't know what you're missing. It's a delicious yogurt made using whole milk and infused with honey, giving it a luxurious velvety, creamy texture and sweet-tart tang taste. Well, this type of yogurt has a slightly thinner texture compared to the strained Greek-style yogurt.

Equipment

- An instant pot

- Thermometer
- Whisk

Ingredients

- ½ gallon of whole milk
- 2 cups of heavy cream
- 4 tablespoons of active yogurt (starter)
- 1 ½ tablespoons of gelatin
- 5 tablespoons of clover honey
- 1/2 cup of household sugar

Directions

Heating the milk and heavy cream

- Ensure the pot is clean, dry, and cool before pouring anything.
- Pour in whole milk and heavy cream, and then cover the pot with the regular lid.
- Push the Yoghurt button. You will need to adjust until the word; "BOIL" appears on the display panel.
- Let the contents heat for about 10 minutes.
- Take the IP lid off and remove the milk skin, and then stir the mixture using a whisk.

- Close the lid and give the mixture time to boil until the IP beeps. Check out if there's any milk skin formed. Make sure to remove it before whisking the milk mixture.
- Measure the temperature of the milk mixture using a digital thermometer. The target temperature is 180°F / 82°C. If the temperature is still below the recommended range, continue heating the milk mixture while closely monitoring the temperature. Heating the milk mixture to achieve the correct temperature should take about 30 minutes.
- Take one cup of warm milk and pour it into a bowl containing gelatin and sugar. Make sure you whisk until gelatin and sugar dissolve completely. Pour this mixture into the hot pot and whist thoroughly.

Cooling the milk mixture

- Unplug the heating unit and carefully remove the inner pot. Place the instant pot in your kitchen sink of cold water.
- Let the temperature drop to 100 - 105 degrees. It should take about 5 to 10

minutes. Don't forget to whisk as it cools down.

- Remove any milk skin.

Inoculating with a yogurt starter

- Place your yogurt starter in a clean, dry bowl and mix it with clover honey.
- Add 4 to 6 tablespoons of the warm milk into the bowl. Whisk the starter mixture until it is smooth.
- Pour the smooth milky starter back into the inner pot and whisk thoroughly.
- Carefully return the inner pot to the IP. You should remove the thermometer and cover the instant pot.

Incubating

- Plugin the heating unit and push the Yogurt button. You will need to adjust the time to 6 hours using the (+) key. Please note that the display panel should display the word "Normal" and not "Less."
- Your Noosa yogurt will be ready after six hours. All that's left is to ladle it into containers or jars and refrigerate the yogurt for about 8-10 hours.

How to Make Viili Yogurt

Viili yogurt comes from Finland and is also known as 'stretchy.' Viili yogurt has a similar consistency as yogurt you buy in the grocery store with a milder taste.

What You Need:

- **Milk** – You can make yogurt from whole milk, 2% skimmed milk or a combination of mil types.
- **Starter culture** – viili yogurt culture or a small portion of viili yogurt containing

live culture. The options available for your starter culture include powdered starter culture, store-bought yogurt, or homemade yogurt from a previous batch.

- **Yogurt Incubator** – The incubator is essential for maintaining your milk and culture mix at about 110 F to 115 F for close to five hours. Therefore, options available to you include a yogurt maker, thermos, or heat keeper jugs. You can also use several mason jars filled with hot water and placed in a cooler.
- **Other requirements** – A large spoon or whisk, storage containers, ladle, mixing bowl.

Directions:

- **Clean all your tools**

It is always advisable to wash and even sterilize all your yogurt, making equipment and surfaces to avoid introducing other unwanted bacteria. Some clean their tools with boiling water, but thorough handwashing is also enough.

- **Start with room temperature milk**

If you're starting with refrigerated milk, you will want to warm the milk to room temperature before adding your yogurt starter culture. This, for me, generally is not a problem, since I tend to use pasteurized box milk from my pantry shelves.

- **Add your starter culture**

When using a yogurt powdered starter, it is okay to whisk it in according to the amount specified on the package instructions.

- **yogurt as a starter culture**

However, when using yogurt as a starter culture, it is advisable to first isolate a small amount of the milk and keep adding it to the starter culture and stir until all of it has been mixed. This is because adding cold yogurt directly to the milk will slow down the incubation by suddenly dropping the temperatures too much.

- **Incubate**

Use your spoon or ladle to transfer the milk and culture mix to your incubator of choice. The primary importance of incubation is to maintain your milk and culture mix at the stated temperature for 5 to 10 hours undisturbed. However, keep in mind that shorter incubation periods under cooler temperatures will produce sweeter, thinner yogurt while longer and hotter incubation periods will produce tarter and thicker yogurt.

- **Checking yogurt for doneness**

When ready, your yogurt should start looking firm. Moreover, it will get more acidic with each passing hour.

- **Store your yogurt**

Once your yogurt is done, store your yogurt in the refrigerator

How to Make Kefir yogurt

You may have noticed a product called kefir appearing on more and more store shelves in recent years as the cultured dairy product has exploded in popularity. Like traditional types of yogurt available in stores, kefir is an excellent probiotic source for the gut, but actually contains a wider variety of good bacteria than traditional yogurt.

Kefir has a thinner consistency than yogurt does, making it easily drinkable without the use of a spoon. It's made by adding kefir grains-- small colonies of bacteria and yeast-- to milk, although it can also be made with water and added to milk alternatives as a lactose-free alternative. Some companies offer various bottled kefir flavors like chocolate and strawberry. Milk kefir can be used to soak flour or to marinate meat, or simply mixed with other drinks. You could also try out some flavorful frozen treats with a healthy kefir base.

Ingredients

- 4 cups of whole milk
- presoftened kefir grains.

Equipment

- a fine-mesh colander
- a glass jar for fermentation
- a ladle
- a stainless-steel pot
- a thermometer
- a water bath
- paper towels, paper coffee filters, or thin fine cloth

Directions

- Clean/sanitize your yogurt equipment, i.e., measuring cups, whisk, spoon, glass jars, etc.
- (Optional, if using room temperature pasteurized milk)
  - Pour milk into the saucepan. Heat gently to 90 degrees Celsius or 195 degrees Fahrenheit. Monitor temperature closely using your thermometer, ensuring the milk doesn't boil.
  - Keep the milk hot for a few minutes (5 minutes) then cool to 40-43 degrees Celsius or 105-110 degrees Fahrenheit
- Add the kefir grains and pour the prepared yogurt milk in the fermentation jar.
- Cover the top with paper towels, paper coffee filter, or thin fine cloth
- Then, secure the cover material tightly with rubber bands.
- Let the kefir milk ferment for around 24 hours in a dark and warm (65 to 85°F / 18 to 29°C) place.
- Once the kefir achieves a thick texture and fermented smell, strain the kefir using a fine-mesh colander and place it in fresh whole milk for future use.
- Once your kefir is done, store your yogurt in the refrigerator

Homemade Icelandic Skyr yogurt

Icelandic Skyr is basically strained skim milk cheese that doubles as a yogurt. It is classified as cheese because it has rennet (complex enzymes used to curdle milk when making cheese). Icelandic Skyr is considered a yogurt solely because of its ultra-thick structure and texture. It has a very rich tangy flavor. Skyr was introduced in the U.S. by an Icelandic expatriate Siggi Hlmarsson hence the name Icelandic Skyr.

Equipment

- A dairy thermometer
- A cheesecloth to drain the curds
- Strainer
- Large bowl
- A saucepan
- Whisk or spoon
- Glass jar and double-walled stainless-steel thermos

Ingredients

- A liter of low-fat milk.
- A tablespoon of Skyr (for bacterial cultures) or yogurt culture
- Rennet

Directions

- Clean/sanitize your yogurt equipment, i.e., measuring cups, whisk, spoon, glass jar, etc.
- Pour milk into the saucepan. Heat gently to 90 degrees Celsius or 195 degrees Fahrenheit. Monitor temperature closely using your thermometer, ensuring the milk doesn't boil.
- Keep the milk hot for a few minutes (5 minutes) then cool to 40-43 degrees Celsius or 105-110 degrees Fahrenheit
- Add the Skyr into the warm milk and mix thoroughly using a whisk or spoon. Yogurt cultures can be used instead. Also, you

can add your rennet if you have some at this step (optional). Rennet adds thickness.

- Keep the mixture at 40 to 50 degrees Celsius for 4 to 5 hours. You can pour the mix into a glass jar and insert the jar into a double-walled stainless-steel thermos to maintain the temperature.
- After approximately 5 hours, the Skyr and whey will have separated. Proceed by lining the strainer using the cheesecloth and place over your bowl.
- Pour the mixture carefully through your cheesecloth and allow to drain. Cover using a lid or plastic wrap to avoid contaminants.
- When the whey has stopped dripping, lift your cheesecloth, and hang your Skyr to drain for 12 hours or more depending on your preferred thickness.

Important

- Depending on your preferences, you can drain the Skyr for longer or less time. Traditionally, Icelandic Skyr is eaten with berries and cream as a dessert. Some people add brown sugar. The Skyr can also be thinned down using water or whey if it is preferred slightly thinner than typical yogurt.

How to Make Yakult

Recently, Yakult yogurt has become popular, majorly thanks to its appearance on a popular program on Netflix.

But what is Yakult yogurt, and why is it gaining popularity?

Well, Yakult yogurt is a probiotic health drink. This Japanese yogurt drink has been around for several decades, and its consumption is known to help build immunity and improve digestion. Yakult yogurt is made from water, skim milk powder, sugar, glucose, Lactobacillus casei shirota, and natural flavors.

Ingredients

- a small bottle of Yakult drink
- ice cubes
- whole milk

Equipment

- a ladle,
- a stainless-steel pot
- a thermometer
- drinking glasses.
- a water bath

Directions

- **Clean all your tools**

Did you know that you actually need a bacterium known as *Lactobacillus bulgaricus* to make good yogurt? Given all the bacteria ever-present around us, it is always advisable to wash and even sterilize all your yogurt making equipment and surfaces to avoid introducing other unwanted bacteria. Some clean their tools with boiling water, but thorough handwashing is also enough.

- **Heat Your Yogurt Milk (optional for pasteurized milk)**

In a stainless-steel or Nonstick pot, heat the milk to 180oF degrees.

Stir the milk frequently to avoid scorching.

Once the temperature has been reached, then turn off the pot and remove the pot.

Additionally, heating the milk for some extra minutes helps in concentrating it so that your yogurt can be thicker.

- **Cool Your Yogurt Milk After heating**

After heating your milk to the boiling point, cool it back down to 110 F-115 F. Make use of your thermometer to track the temperatures. Also, keep stirring to ensure even cooling.

- **Add your starter culture**

When using a yogurt powdered starter, it is okay to whisk it in according to the amount specified on the package instructions.

However, when using yogurt as a starter culture, it is advisable to first isolate a small amount of the milk and keep adding it to the starter culture and stir until all of it has been mixed. This is because adding cold yogurt directly to the milk will slow down the incubation by suddenly dropping the temperatures too much.

- **Incubate**

Use your spoon or ladle to transfer the milk
and culture mix to your incubation method of
choice. The primary importance of incubation
is to maintain your milk and culture mix at the
stated temperature for 12 to 14 hours
undisturbed.

- **Store your yogurt**

Once your yogurt is done, move the yogurt
into sealable serving glasses and store your
yogurt in the refrigerator

How to Make Instant Pot Yogurt

Step One: Clean Your Instant Pot

This may sound like a real no brainer, but a quick wash may leave residue in your instant pot that will affect the flavor of your yogurt. Sanitizing your pot will help you get all the natural tastes from your finished product.

Pour boiling water into the inner pot and leave for 10 minutes. Discard the water and remove residual moisture with a kitchen towel.

Step Two: Preparation

Take ½ gallon of your preferred milk. You can use low-fat options, but you will get the best results from full-fat organic milk. Remove the preferred milk from the refrigerator 2 hours before you start to make the yogurt for optimum results.

Pour the preferred milk into the inner pot of the instant pot pressure cooker. Replace the lid and press the button that says yogurt, adjust until you hit the function boil. The vent on the cooker can be left sealed or unsealed during the process as you are not using pressure to cook.

When the process has completed, the machine will beep to indicate your yogurt is ready. Remove the lid and test the temperature with a thermometer to make sure the liquid has reached 180°F / 82°C degrees.

You can then remove the inner pot to let the mixture cool but leave it in the Instant Pot for an extra five minutes as this will give you a thicker consistency.

Step Three: Cool the Yogurt

The mixture needs to be cooled to around 105-115 degrees. This can take an hour or so when left on a counter to cool naturally. To accelerate the cooling process, place the inner pot in a larger bowl, and surround it with ice or iced water. This will shorten the process to around 15 minutes.

Step Four: Remove the Top Layer of Your Milk

Now it's time to remove the skin from your liquid. Skin is formed when milk is heated; the protein and fat molecules clump together and condense on the surface. Removing this soft protein layer will help you get creamier results. The degree to which milk forms a skin is dependent on the type of milk you use for your yogurt.

Step Five: Add a Yogurt Starter

The easiest way to add a starter to your yogurt is to use prepared yogurt with plain and live cultures. If you add a yogurt that contains any type of sweetener or doesn't have live yogurt cultures, your recipe will not work!

You can buy yogurt starters to produce high-quality probiotic results, but the choices can be overwhelming.

Here are some of the best brands to consider:

- Euro Cuisine All-Natural Starter Culture: Possibly the best product on the market this kit contains 10 packets of 5 grams of culture. Each packet makes 20 jars of homemade yogurt. The results are smooth and creamy with a classic tangy yogurt taste. Reviews from customers show that they found the instructions easy to follow and produce a taste, unlike store-bought yogurts.
- Yogourmet 16 pack Starter: This product is aimed at customers who appreciate a value pack and don't want to pay over the odds. It contains only natural ingredients and all the live cultures your body needs. Available in

single batch packs or as a budget 16 pack option, you can try before you commit to the brand.

▪ Cultures for Health Vegan Option Yogurt Starter, which is made for use with coconut, soy, cashew, or rice milk, this super healthy option allows vegans to enjoy a non-dairy variety of yogurt that is huge on taste. Based on customer reviews, this product offers an affordable way to make healthy vegan yogurt that tastes great.

▪ Greek Traditional Yogurt Kit: For all lovers of the thick creamy Greek yogurt, this kit provides the user with the means to make traditional Greek yogurt traditionally. It includes a cheesecloth and thickener for you to produce a fool-proof product that tastes better than any store-bought option!

Step Six: Allowing Your Yogurt to Incubate

Now place your inner pot back in your Instant Pot with the lid on. Once again, the valve position is irrelevant. Hit the button marked yogurt and adjust the timer until it reads 8 hours. The Instant pot will then turn your gloopy mixture into creamy smooth yogurt for you to enjoy.

Step Seven: Transfer and Enjoy!

Take the yogurt from the inner pot and put it in containers. Transfer to the refrigerator and serve when required.

But wait! What happens if your Instant Pot doesn't have a yogurt button?

How can you possibly use it to make your own delicious yogurt? Well, it is a bit trickier, but it can be done.

You will need a suitable thermometer and a couple of towels for the process, but that's all the extra equipment required.

- Pour your ½ gallon of preferred milk into the inner pot.
- Turn on the Sauté function; this could also be labeled as sear or heat.
- Heat the milk to 180°F degrees. Stir the milk frequently to avoid it scorching

- Once the temperature has been reached then turn off the pressure cooker and remove the inner pot
- Cool in the same way as the above method until the liquid is 108 degrees precisely
- Now use your preferred starting option and mix until it's properly incorporated.
- Replace the inner pot back into the Instant Pot and place the lid back on
- Take the two towels and wrap around the Instant Pot to form an incubation chamber.
- Leave for 10 hours and then transfer your homemade yogurt to the refrigerator.

How to Make Fat Free Yogurt With Your Instant Pot

If you don't want to make your yogurt with full-fat milk, the best way to make it healthier is to use a fat-free yogurt as a starter. For you ½ gallon of skim milk, add 3 tbsp of nonfat yogurt as a starter.

You will find the liquid has more water than the full-fat version, but this is not a problem.

Simply drain the excess water and discard it. As the yogurt sits in the refrigerator, more liquid will form on the top. Just mix it back into the yogurt before serving.

How to Make Greek Yogurt Without the Specialist Starter Kit

If you prefer your yogurt to be thick and creamy, it is simple to get this effect. Use a clean cheesecloth or alternative material to cover a strainer. Position the strainer over a large mixing bowl and add the yogurt to the cloth. You may need to strain your yogurt in batches depending on the amount of yogurt you have. Let the yogurt drain for 8 hours or overnight, if possible. Once the process has finished, remove the thick creamy yogurt from the cheesecloth and put it in pots. The cheesecloth can be washed and reused or thrown in the trash.

Alternatives to Cheesecloth

- ⬚ Cotton fabric: A pillowcase, bandana, cloth napkin or jelly bag
- ⬚ Fine mesh bag: Laundry bag, mesh bag, or a paint strainer bag can work

better than cheesecloth if you plan on making lots of yogurts. Pick these items up from your local hardware store for an alternative that is more durable and easier to clean

▢ Pantyhose: Create the perfect strainer by using a clean pair of tights or pantyhose to drain your cheese into. Simply toss them into the wash after, and they are good to go!

▢ Coffee Filter: You can use the paper disposable ones, but they may disintegrate. The reusable one that comes with the coffee machine will serve you better for yogurt straining.

When you have strained your yogurt, you will find you have excess whey in your cheesecloth. You can use this in smoothies or shakes to add protein to your diet.

Chapter 10: How to Make Yogurt Cheese at Home

Making cheese is so easy that you can do all of the prep work in just a few minutes, and yogurt cheese is something not commonly found at your local grocery store.

What is yogurt cheese?

Yogurt cheese is a step beyond Greek yogurt and is yogurt that is strained to thicken until the strained yogurt has a consistency to cream cheese.

How to make yogurt cheese at home?

- Start with 1 cup or more of yogurt and make sure that it is real yogurt with live active cultures.
- Take a strainer or funnel and line it with either a coffee filter or two layers of cheesecloth. Actually, I use a clean square of an old white teeshirt. The cloth will allow the liquid to drain away while leaving the yogurt behind.
- Fill the funnel or stainer with the yogurt.
- Using plastic cover the funnel or strainer.
- Place a strainer, sieve, or funnel over a large bowl with clearance space to catch the drained liquid.
- Put the strainer or funnel, with the bowl under it into your refrigerator. Let yogurt set in the strainer for at least a day, longer if you want your yogurt cheese thicker. I usually check and empty the catch bowl a few times to keep too much liquid from accumulating. The longer your yogurt cheese sits in your refrigerator, the thicker it will become.

- That's it; now you can remove your yogurt cheese and store your yogurt cheese in a sealed container in the refrigerator.

Storing Yogurt Cheese

Once your yogurt cheese is finished, make sure that you keep it refrigerated. It is a dairy product, so leaving it out at room temperature for a lengthy period will cause the yogurt cheese to spoil. You should also use the yogurt cheese you've made within about a week. Any longer and it could spoil.

How to Use Yogurt Cheese?

Yogurt cheese has a myriad of uses, perhaps, the easiest way to take advantage of your homemade yogurt cheese is to use it as a substitute for cream cheese. This is especially true for icebox or no-bake recipes such as cheesecake. Whenever you are making a flavored recipe, yogurt cheese may also be substituted for cottage cheese or ricotta cheese. In the case of cottage cheese or ricotta cheese, the flavor and texture may be slightly different. Most any recipe that calls for a creamy soft cheese is a candidate to consider using yogurt cheese as a substitute.

Also, having yogurt cheese around and using as a substitute allows you not to have to make a run to the store and specifically purchase cream cheese as a grocery item.

Chapter 11: Tips for Cooking with Yogurt

If you're consuming your yogurt in its raw form, it's time to experiment with it in various recipes. Yogurt can be used to cook several savory and sweet dishes and can be used as an ingredient in a variety of meals. You might not know it yet, but yogurt is one of the most underrated and valuable food items that sit modestly in your refrigerator. It is a simple ingredient that can turn any plain food into a moist meal with lots of texture. In this chapter, we'll show you a few ways to cook with yogurt and use it as an important ingredient in versatile meals.

Yogurt Cream

Yogurt cream is a healthier version of whipped cream with the majority of its goodness and deliciousness. It's the best version of your yogurt, as well. Yogurt cream is basically whipped yogurt. The taste is almost like a tangier version of normal yogurt but is light, fluffy, and creamy. Greek yogurt is commonly used to make yogurt cream because it is rich in fat content and thicker consistency. It stands between yogurt and whipped cream.

To make yogurt cream, you will need 8 ounces of plain Greek yogurt, 6 ounces of heavy cream, 3 tablespoons of honey or maple syrup, ¼ teaspoon vanilla extract, and a pinch of salt. You will need a mixer with a whisk attachment to mix it. Put all these ingredients in a large bowl and mix thoroughly using the mixer at a low speed, gradually elevating it. Whisk it for five minutes and until the mixture becomes a bit fluffy. Transfer to a serving bowl and chill it.

Yogurt cream is a fantastic ingredient for desserts, especially when topped with berries or any sliced fruit, or for parfaits. You need to consume yogurt cream within two to four days of preparing it to enjoy its consistency and flavor to the maximum.

Yogurt Oatmeal

Oatmeal is a health and easy recipe to kick-start your morning. Paired with healthy ingredients, it can be quite filling and help in maintaining your weight. If that's your goal, you should use Greek yogurt that's high in protein content or skim milk yogurt that offers low-fat content. To make oatmeal with yogurt, you need to boil ½ cup of oats with a little bit of water and pour the oats into a bowl. Add two tablespoons of yogurt, ½ tablespoon of peanut butter, some sliced fruit or berries, and top it with chia seeds. You have a healthy breakfast with minimal effort.

Replace Mayonnaise with Yogurt in Salads

Mayonnaise is considered an unhealthy ingredient that can completely ruin your diet. A lot of people use yogurt in salads as a dressing to add extra flavor to boring veggies. However, it only adds a lot of calories to the meal. You can easily substitute full-fat traditional yogurt or Greek yogurt for mayonnaise in your salads. If you can't let go of mayonnaise because of its distinct taste, you can just add one tiny spoon of mayonnaise and swap the rest with yogurt. Add extra ingredients such as herbs and garlic to increase the flavor of the salad.

Use Yogurt as a Marinade

Yogurt is used as a base for the marinating of fish and chicken, or any preferred meat. The flavors of your ingredients, such as lemon juice and spices, will infuse into the meat through yogurt because it will stick to the meat's surface. This will give you more flavor and texture. To make the marinade, you can use simple ingredients such as Greek yogurt, olive oil, lime juice, garlic, fresh herbs, mustard, salt, pepper, and any spices of your choice. Bathe the meat thoroughly in the marinade and cover it with a lid. Leave it in the refrigerator for a few hours for the meat to fully soak the flavors. After a while, roast or grill the meat as per the recipe you're using.

Yogurt Can Be Used for Dips

Yogurt is great for dips. It provides a creamy base and accepts all kinds of ingredients to make amazing sauces and dips. It's also a great alternative for sour cream. Just dip your baked potatoes, quesadillas, fries, and tacos in a yogurt dip to get a creamy and tangy flavor.

There are many ways to use yogurt in cooking. You can also use it as a sauce, a marinade, or a dip. The best part is, yogurt goes well with almost any kind of meal and ingredients.

Chapter 12: Making Flavored Yogurt and Honey Yogurt

Now that we've learned all major aspects of yogurt-making with the exact procedure, it's time to add some fun to it. In this chapter, we'll be talking about flavored yogurt and how you can easily make it at home. Store-bought flavored yogurt can be full of harmful preservatives and sweeteners that are detrimental to your health in the long run. So, why not make it at home? With a minimum of effort, you can prepare healthy and delicious flavored yogurt options using fresh ingredients and no additional preservatives.

Experimenting with Different Flavors

Let's try a few flavor varieties that can make for a delightful dessert that's extremely healthy for your family. You can either add toppings such as berries, kiwis, sliced bananas, or peach on top of fresh yogurt along with some maple syrup or serve it by mixing in some jam or fruit sauce. To make flavored yogurt, first, prepare plain yogurt as instructed in the previous chapters. You can prepare a reduction of a fruit of your choice using sugar and some warm water, or make some marmalade. Add a few drops of this reduction in the yogurt and mix it until it forms an even consistency.

Here are a few more flavored yogurt recipes to experiment with when it's time for dessert:

• A mocha-flavored yogurt will be enjoyed by most adults! For this, you'll need 1 teaspoon of instant coffee, 1 tablespoon of rich cocoa powder, 2 tablespoons of maple syrup, 1 serving of fresh homemade yogurt, and 1 teaspoon of warm water. Mix all the flavored yogurt ingredients together and serve chilled. This will give you an instant kick of coffee and chocolate yogurt, similar to the store-bought alternatives.

• We hardly know any person who doesn't like vanilla-flavored yogurt. To make vanilla-flavored yogurt, you'll need 1 cup of unflavored full-fat or Greek yogurt, 1 teaspoon of maple syrup, and ½ teaspoon of pure vanilla extract. Mix them together until the texture and color are even. Serve chilled. You can also use vanilla-flavored yogurt as a base for smoothies.

• Summertime calls for some mango-flavored dessert. And what's better than mango yogurt? To make this, you'll need ½ cup of fresh mango puree, a few chopped mangoes, 1 cup of unflavored full-fat or Greek yogurt, and 1 teaspoon of maple syrup (optional). Mix them together until the texture and color are even. Add the mango pieces on top to garnish and serve chilled.

Making Honey Yogurt

Honey yogurt is another classic flavor that never fails to please. Honey yogurt is also a healthy alternative for those who are trying to cut back on sugar and watching their weight. To make this, you'll need 4 cups of unflavored full-fat or Greek yogurt, 3 tablespoons of honey, and ¼ teaspoon of orange-flower water. Mix them well until the texture is even. We'd recommend making this recipe and storing it in your refrigerator constantly for regular use as a cooking ingredient.

Flavoring yogurt is an excellent way to work some nutrition in your kids' diet while satisfying their palates at the same time. Try these flavors today, and we're sure they'll be part of your weekly meal plans.

Chapter 13 - Making Yogurt Ice Cream At Home

It's a scorching hot day, and your body is yearning for something cold and sweet, but your mind is craving something healthier than ice cream. What should you do? Well, your dilemma is solved now. Make yourself and your loved ones yogurt ice cream! Yogurt ice cream, also known as frozen yogurt, is a great healthy treat for anyone that is looking to cut back on their calorie consumption, but not looking to cut back on flavor.

What is Yogurt Ice Cream?

Yogurt ice cream, commonly known as frozen yogurt, is a combination of three key ingredients: yogurt, milk, and sweetener. You may say well yogurt ice cream is just putting your yogurt in the freezer and voila! You have yogurt ice cream. The steps to make yogurt ice cream are easy to follow.

How Long Does Yogurt Ice Cream Take to Make?

Making yogurt ice cream typically takes around 45 minutes to prepare and around 4 hours until you're able to consume it because of the freezing time. Typically, you'll want to make it the night before you want to eat it.

Health Benefits of Yogurt Ice Cream

Yogurt ice cream is loaded with essential nutrients. Yogurt ice cream contains probiotics. Probiotics are live bacteria that are great for your digestive system. Their main job is to prevent harmful bacteria from staying in your digestive tract. Yogurt ice cream is also full of protein. Protein is great for those who are building muscle mass and looking to speed up their metabolism. It's great for those who are looking to lose weight. Protein also helps the body burn fat. But the benefits don't stop here! Yogurt ice cream also contains calcium, potassium vitamin B12, and B2 magnesium. If you add fruit to your ice cream yogurt, you will have even more vitamins.

Yogurt ice cream can also help to protect your body from major sicknesses. Research has shown that there's a link between the consumption of calcium and a decreased chance of cardiovascular disease. So not only is calcium good for your bones, it's a great way to protect your body from illness and disease.

Magnesium, which is found in yogurt ice cream, can help stabilize your blood sugar and assist your body's immune system. If you have problems with constipation, magnesium can assist with normal bowel movements again. Magnesium also works wonders for your mind! Studies have shown magnesium consumption can help prevent panic attacks, anxiety, and stress.

Potassium in yogurt ice cream can do marvelous things for your body. Potassium is wonderful for brain health and heart health. It can also decrease your chances of having a stroke. Potassium plays a major role in your body, and what better way to consume potassium than in a tasty treat like yogurt ice cream.

Vitamin B2, also known as riboflavin, found in yogurt ice cream, gives your body miraculous benefits. Vitamin B2 is known to increase your energy. Riboflavin breaks down protein fats, carbohydrates, and protein. B2 is great for your skin.

Overall, yogurt ice cream is very beneficial for your body and mind. The health benefits are only effective if you consume in moderation. So, although frozen yogurt is delicious, remember not to binge on it – trust me, you may be tempted too!

Yogurt Ice Cream vs. Regular Ice Cream

The main difference between yogurt ice cream and regular ice cream is the elimination of the cream in yogurt ice cream. Instead of using a cream that is high in fat, yogurt ice cream uses yogurt instead.

Flavor Difference

Ice cream flavors and yogurt ice cream flavors are mostly the same. The main difference is ice cream manufactures tend to use artificial flavoring in cream, whereas if you were to make homemade yogurt ice cream, you could use more natural flavors. Also, yogurt ice cream can be a tad bit tarter than regular ice cream.

Which One is Better for Your Health?

Yogurt ice cream helps your digestive system because it contains probiotics, unlike regular ice cream. Yogurt ice cream also helps you lose weight, whereas regular ice cream helps you pack on the pounds. Ice cream has more fat, whereas yogurt ice cream has more protein. Together they both have vitamins and minerals that assist with a lot of health issues. Yogurt ice cream contains fewer calories than regular ice cream. Also, yogurt ice cream contains half the amount of fats than regular ice cream. If you have just had a workout and you're looking to indulge in something sweet, you can eat yogurt ice cream to get a little protein boost and satisfy your sweet tooth.

Frozen Yogurt History

Regular ice cream has been undefeated in the world of sweet dairy products. Still, yogurt ice cream is creating competition to dethrone regular ice cream as America's primary go-to cold dairy treat. Yogurt ice cream is healthier and is more lactose friendly. In recent times, many frozen yogurt shops have sprouted up in every city, and these popular shops are giving traditional ice cream stores some friendly competition.

Where Did Yogurt Ice Cream Come From?

Before it became the most popular frozen dairy product in recent times, some form yogurt ice cream had been around for a remarkable 5,000 years! Yogurt was created around 4,900 years ago in both the Middle East and India. People there have used yogurt for many different foods. In 1970 H.P. Hood introduced frozen yogurt. He called it "frogurt" and served it as a delicious dessert. People enjoyed it because it tasted so much like ice cream. Icecream Company TCBY (This Can't Be Yogurt) saw that the masses were in the market for a healthier product that still tasted like ice cream. So, they made a business plan and opened their first frozen yogurt shop in 1981, and now there are over 1,000 frozen yogurt shops nationwide.

Why Should You Eat Yogurt Ice Cream?

There are many different reasons why you should eat yogurt ice cream, and here are some. Yogurt ice cream is simply "what's in." It's a very trendy dessert as most people are becoming more health conscience in their dessert choices. Most states in America, especially California, are saying out with junk food and in with organic/natural foods. Another reason to eat yogurt ice cream is that it is so easy to make. Impress your friends and have them thinking, "Wow, I didn't know you could cook!" Making homemade yogurt ice cream is an awesome way to have a treat with your family. Get everyone involved. Invite your kids into the kitchen and create memories that will be cherished forever.

Besides the social benefits of yogurt ice cream, the reason you should eat it lies in its health benefits. Yogurt ice cream is a perfect substitute for regular ice cream. Instead of gravitating to an unhealthy snack that is full of empty calories, turn toward yogurt ice cream, and reap the health benefits. It's full of vitamins B12, B2, probiotics, calcium, minerals, potassium, and magnesium.

If you are starting a diet soon, you should consider implementing a healthy dessert such as yogurt ice cream. Maybe your children are refusing to eat fruit. Bamboozle them by giving them yogurt ice cream. They will never know the difference. In fact, they will say it tastes even better than ice cream. The yogurt ice cream industry (frozen yogurt) is booming. If you have a creative mind, make a recipe that will be irresistible to everyone and start your own business. Before you start buying heavy machinery, start small. Come up with a unique flavor and let your friends try it. If it's a success, expand to people outside your friends (maybe they were too nice) and get others to test it. Then you can create a unique brand that is catchy and trendy and start small by making a stand or buying a truck and parking outside of your local university. Begin to sell it to the students. If it's successful, move to the next level and open a small shop. If that's a huge deal, think about manufacturing it. Go for it!

Ingredients Needed to Make Yogurt Ice Cream

Ingredients:

- Plain Greek Yogurt: Plain Greek yogurt has a lot of health benefits. It includes less sugar and more protein than regular yogurt.
- Vanilla Extract: To get the best results, use real vanilla extract rather than artificial.
- Powdered Sweetener: Look for a sweetener that has the least number of calories.
- Unsweetened Cocoa Powder: The most common brand to find in the store is Hershey's Natural Unsweetened Cocoa.

Measurements:

- 2 cups of Greek plain yogurt
- ½ cup of unsweetened cocoa powder
- 1 teaspoon of vanilla extract
- ½ cup of powdered sweetener

Steps

- Simply take your ingredients and put them in a bowl together and blend. Use a food processor for the best results, but if you don't have a food processor, a blender will work too.
- Then place plastic wrap on top of the bowl and put it in the freezer.
- Keep in the freezer for about 1hr and 45 minutes then mix it.
- After mixing put it back into the freezer

Strawberry Ice Cream Yogurt Recipe

Ingredients:

- 2 cups frozen strawberries
- ¼ cup plain Greek yogurt
- 1/4 Tablespoon fresh lemon juice
- 2 Tablespoons fresh honey

Directions:

- Take all the ingredients and mix them in a food processor.
- Mix all your ingredients for about 3 to 4 minutes.
- Place your ice cream yogurt into a new container that has a lid. You can also use a bowl and just put plastic wrap on the top.
- Store in the freezer for about 6 hours.
- Note: To make any other yogurt ice cream involving fruit, just replace the strawberries in the recipe with a fruit of your choice.

Raspberry Sorbet Ice Cream Yogurt

Ingredients:

- 2 cups of pure sugar (Granulated)
- 2cups of water
- 5 and ¾ cups of frozen raspberries that have been thawed out
- A pinch of salt
- Plain Greek yogurt

Directions:

- Make a sugar-water syrup by adding both to a medium pan set over medium-low heat.
- Cook the mixture until the sugar has fully disappeared.
- Then add all the ingredients and mix it using a food processor.
- Put it in the freezer for around 2 hours. Make sure you have the yogurt ice cream airtight in the freezer so ice crystals will not form.
- After two hours, take the Raspberry Sorbet out and mix it again.
- Put it back in the freezer for 3 hours.

Coffee Yogurt Ice Cream

Ingredients:

- 2 cups of any kind of milk. Choose your preference.
- 1 ¾ cups of sugar
- 2 eggs - whisked
- A pinch of salt
- 1 ½ cups of plain Greek yogurt
- A teaspoon of vanilla

- 2 tablespoons of coffee shots

Directions:

- Pour your milk into a pan and then cook the milk over low heat. Keep the milk below the boiling point.
- Remove milk pan from heat and add in sugar, stirring until it dissolves.
- Dump the milk mixture over the beaten eggs, stirring it until the mixture well blended.
- Transfer blended mixture to the top of a double boiler and cook, constantly stirring, until thick and smooth.
- Cool the mixture to room temperature
- Add remaining ingredients and mix thoroughly.
- Put it in the freezer and chill for 2-4 hours.

Chapter 14: Ideas For Using Your Yogurt

Here are a few additional ideas you can try with your newly fermented yogurt.

Traditional Greek Tzatziki Recipe

What is Tzatziki?

Greek traditional Tzatziki recipes are super simple to make and taste great with almost anything. Tzatziki, although it is traditionally Greek, is enjoyed across the Mediterranean, Turkey, and the Middle East. Tzatziki is easily made with fresh, natural yogurt, cucumber, olive oil, herbs, garlic, lemon, and sea salt.

Ways to Enjoy Tzatziki

You can enjoy Tzatziki with a range of fresh, grilled, or roasted vegetables such as bell peppers, carrots, mushrooms, corn, asparagus, and more.

You can also enjoy Tzatziki with a range of sandwiches, falafel, salads, gyros, pitas, and kebabs.

Tzatziki also makes for a great appetizer, served alone or alongside hummus with crisp fresh vegetables, toasted pita, or breadsticks.

Ingredients

- 1 1/4 cups of unflavored Greek yogurt
- 1 pressed or minced clove of garlic
- 1 tbs of lemon juice
- 1/4 teaspoon of fine sea salt

- 2 cups of grated fresh cucumber, you do not need to seed or peel the cucumber
- 2 tbs of chopped fresh mint, you can also add a sprinkle of dill
- 2 tbs of extra virgin olive oil

Directions

- Grate your cucumber into even fresh strips and then drain them, removing any excess liquid by lightly squeezing them a handful at a time before transferring to a mixing bowl.
- Then spoon in the yogurt, stirring lightly and add the lemon, garlic, herbs, and salt. Mix thoroughly and evenly and let it all sit for 5 to 10 minutes to allow the flavors to blend. (after 5 minutes taste and test, we didn't find we needed to add more seasoning, but it is to your taste)
- Incorporate one tablespoon of olive oil and then drizzle the second.
- Your Tzatziki can be enjoyed immediately or will keep up to 4 days in a sealed container in the fridge.

Lime Yogurt Gelatin Dessert

Ingredients

For Gelatin

- 1 package unflavored gelatin (1 tablespoon / 0.3 oz)
- 1 package sugar-free lime gelatin (0.6 oz / 17g)
- ½ cup (120 ml) cold water
- 3 ½ cups boiling water
- 3/4 cup (180 ml) plain, full-fat or Greek yogurt
- 3/4 cup (180 ml) heavy cream

For Garnish

- Whipped cream (optional)
- Slice of Lime per serving (optional)

Directions

- Measure, cover, and let the yogurt warm to about room temperature.
- Bloom your gelatin by putting spreading both packets evenly over the cold water and letting the gelatin soften. I usually do this in the mixing bowl, where I intend to dissolve the gelatin with hot water.
- Heat the remaining water. To speed up preparation and reduce the supervision required, I usually heat my water in the microwave in a large microwave-safe glass measuring cup.

- Combine the boiling water with the bloomed gelatin and stir until completely dissolved.
- Set aside the dissolved gelatin let the gelatin to cool down to warm room temperature; about 30 minutes. Do not refrigerate the gelatin or the gelatin may set; especially, you get distracted by life for a few more minutes than planned.
- When the gelatin mixture cold to room temperature, whisk in the yogurt until evenly combined.
- Divide the mixture into serving contains or an appropriately sized serving dish if serving the gelatin family-style.
- Refrigerate the gelatin until set, about 3 hours or more.
- When serving, If desired, garnish with whipping cream and a slice of lime.

How To Serve

- The gelatin is best served cold.

Alternatives

- For richer gelatin replace yogurt with 3/4 cup (180 ml) plain, full-fat or Greek

Albert L Swope

yogurt and 3/4 cup (180 ml) heavy cream, mixed together.
- You make this work with any flavor gelatin, which your family likes, but you may also want to change the garnish, as well.

Cook's Notes

- We make our own yogurt and the way I make yogurt; the yogurt is nearly as thick as Greek yogurt.
- If you want to skip the unflavored gelatin, then reduce the hot water from 3 ½ cups to 2 ¾ cups, and you should be fine. I use the because I want the full batch, and the unflavored gelatin also adds a measure of safety, ensuring the gelatin will set and be firm.
- It is important to let the dissolved gelatin cool, so don't run it. If the gelatin is to heat, it will kill the living yogurt culture, which gives this dessert some health benefits.
- We always leave plenty of space at the top of the dish to have room for lots of whipped cream.

Servings

- Makes 11-12 half-cup servings

Quick Yogurt Bread

Ingredients

- 7.5 oz plain Greek Yogurt
- 1 cup of sugar
- 2 cups all-purpose flour
- 1 tbsp baking powder
- 1 tsp baking soda
- ½ tsp salt
- 2 eggs
- 1 tsp vanilla extract

Directions

- Preheat the oven to 350 degrees F.
- Grease loaf pan with butter/cooking spray and line with parchment paper
- Combine the dry ingredients (flour, baking powder, baking soda, and salt) in a medium-size bowl and set aside.
- Mix yogurt, sugar, eggs, and vanilla extract with hand whisk/hand mixer thoroughly. Add in flour mixture a little at a time to avoid lumps. Mix well until the mixture is smooth without lumps. Do not overmix
- Pour mixture into loaf pan.

- Bake for 45 minutes until light golden brown and an inserted toothpick comes out clean.

Servings

- Makes 1 – 9 x 4-inch loaf pan, about 9 servings

Cook's Notes:

- Feel free to use any yogurt of your choice
- Use chocolate chip, raisins, seeds, nuts for toppings if desired

Banana Yogurt Muffins

Ingredients

	US measure	Metric measure
Low-fat vanilla yogurt	1 cup	240 ml
Vegetable oil	¼ cup	50 ml
Low-fat milk	2	10 ml

	teaspoons	
Flour	2 cups	480 ml
Baking powder	1 tablespoon	5 ml
Ground cinnamon	¼ teaspoon	1.25 ml
Sugar	½ cup	120 ml
Salt	½ teaspoon	2.5 ml
Banana	2 ripe	
Eggs	1	

Directions

- Start and preheat oven to 400 degrees F (200 degrees C).
- Prepare muffin pan with nonstick vegetable spray.
- Cut the ripe bananas into small pieces and keep aside. Don't mash them
- In a small mixing bowl, lightly beat the egg.
- Add the milk, yogurt, and vegetable oil. Stir the mixture until well combined.

- Combine the flour, cinnamon, sugar, and salt in a large mixing bowl
- Slowing pour the wet mixture into the dry mixture and lightly stir with a rubber spatula.
- Add the chopped bananas and stir gently.
- Fill muffin cups with the batter to 2/3 full
- Bake for 15-20 minutes and insert a toothpick into the center of one muffin. If it comes out clean, it's ready.
- Remove the muffins from the oven
- Place the banana yogurt muffins on a cooling rack for at least 5 minutes.

Servings

- This recipe is for 12 servings.

How best to serve the dish?

- Serve warm with hot tea or your favorite drink.

How to store

- Allow muffins to cool completely—store muffins in an airtight container. Line the base with a paper towel and cover the muffins with another paper towel to soak up the moisture. Put muffins in a freezer bag and store them in the freezer.

How long can it be stored?

- Muffins in airtight containers can last up to 4 days and up to 3 months when they are frozen.

Chilled Eggplant Yogurt Salad

Ingredients

- 1 cup plain yogurt
- 1/2 teaspoons salt
- 1/3 cup green onions, with tops, minced
- 1/4 teaspoon pepper
- 12 grape tomatoes washed and halved (optional, for garnish)
- 2 medium eggplants (about 2 pounds), peeled and cut in 1-inch chunks
- 2 tablespoons olive oil

- 5 tablespoons lemon juice (juice of about 2 lemons)
- medium clove of garlic, crushed (optional)

Directions

- In a saucepan, bring 6 cups water, 2 tablespoons lemon juice, and 1 teaspoon salt to a boil.
- Add the eggplants; cover, and simmer until tender, about 7 minutes.
- Drain and cool.
- In a bowl, combine the eggplants, remaining 3 tablespoons lemon juice, green onions, oil, remaining h teaspoon salt, pepper, and garlic; and mix well.
- Stir in the yogurt just until blended.
- Chill.
- Divide salad and plate servings and garnish with tomato wedges, if you wish.

Servings

- Makes 4 to 6 servings

Crustless Zucchini Quiche For Two

This Zucchini Quiche is another FODMAP friendly recipe, which makes a nice breakfast or dinner.

Total Time

- 45 Minutes

Ingredients

- 1 teaspoon, Cooking Oil
- 4 ¼ ounces, Zucchini
- 4 ¼ ounces, Canned Mushrooms (drained)

- ½ Medium, Yellow Bell Pepper (chopped)
- 1 teaspoon, Salt & Black Pepper or to taste
- ½ teaspoon, Paprika (ground)
- ½ teaspoon, Mixed Italian Herbs
- 6 cups, Baby Spinach (fresh)
- 6 1/3 ounces, Smoked Chicken Breast (chopped)
- 4 Eggs
- 3 ½ ounces, Plain Greek Yogurt (lactose-free)
- 2 1/8 ounces, Cheddar Cheese (shredded, Divided Into Portions)

Directions

- Turn on the oven and preheat at to 350°F (175°C)
- Grease a quiche pan and set aside.
- At medium heat, preheat cooking oil in a large frying pan and add the zucchini, mushrooms, bell pepper, salt, pepper, paprika, and Italian herbs.
- Stir well and cook for 2 minutes
- Add the spinach, smoked chicken breast, and cook for another 2 minutes until the spinach has wilted.
- Take off the heat and transfer to the greased quiche pan. Set aside.

- In a mixing bowl, whisk the eggs and Greek yogurt together.
- Stir in half of the cheese and then pour the mixture on top of the veggie mix.
- Evenly spread the remaining cheese over the quiche and transfer to the oven.
- Bake for about 20 – 25 minutes, or until a toothpick inserted comes out clean.
- Divide between plates and enjoy.

Servings

- This recipe makes two servings

No-bake Yogurt Cheesecake

Ingredients

For Crust

- 1 ½ cup crushed graham crackers
- 1 stick and 2 tbsp butter, melted
- 1 ½ tbsp sugar

For Filling

- 8 oz cream cheese, softened
- 8 oz plain Greek yogurt
- ½ cup of sugar

- 1 envelope gelatin powder (0.25 oz)
- ½ cup hot water
- 1 tsp vanilla extract

Directions

For Crust

- Grease pie pan with butter.
- Put graham crackers, melted butter, and sugar in the food processor.
- Pulse, mix thoroughly.
- Press evenly into the bottom of the pan, also the side. Chill in the freezer until needed. Set aside

For Filling

- Add hot water into the measuring cup, add in the gelatin powder.
- Stir for 1 minute or until powder is completely dissolved. Set aside.
- In a medium-size bowl, combine sugar and cream cheese.
- Mix thoroughly using a mixer until smooth and creamy.
- Add in Greek yogurt and vanilla extract, then continue mixing for 1 minute.
- Add in gelatin mixture and mix again until just combined, for 10-15 seconds.

Pour cream cheese mixture to the prepared pan.

- Chill the yogurt cheesecake in the fridge at least 3 hours before serving.

Servings

- Makes 1 – 9-inch diameter pie pan; about 8 slices

Cook's Notes

- Cheesecake can be prepped in advance

No-Bake Yogurt Peach Pie

Ingredients

For Crust

- 1 ½ cup crushed graham crackers
- 1 stick and 2 tbsp butter, melted
- 1 ½ tbsp sugar

For Filling

- 2 oz cream cheese, softened
- ½ cup of sugar
- 4 oz plain Greek Yogurt
- 2 oz cool whip
- 7 oz peaches, liquified in a blender
- 1 envelope gelatin powder (0,25 oz)
- ½ cup hot water
- More peach slices for garnish
- Strawberries for garnish

Directions

For Crust

- Grease pie pan with butter.
- Combine sugar, graham crackers, and melted butter in the food processor.
- Mix thoroughly.
- Press evenly into the bottom of the pan, also the side.
- Chill in the freezer until needed. Set aside

For Filling

- Add hot water into the measuring cup, add in the gelatin powder. Stir for 1 minute or until powder is completely dissolved. Set aside.
- In a medium-size bowl, combine the sugar and cream cheese, then mix together using a hand mixer until creamy and smooth.
- Add in yogurt, cool whip, and peach juice, continue mixing until well-combined.
- Add in gelatin mixture and mix for another 10-15 seconds or until just combined.
- Pour over the prepared pie pan, chill in the freezer for at least 3 hours or until firm.

Servings

- Makes 1 – 9-inch pie pan; about 8 servings

Cook's Notes

- Pie can be prepped in advance
- For more fun crust, substitute graham crackers, with oreo cookies, or any other crackers, cookies, or just about dry cereal of your choice
- Peaches also can be substituted with any fruit of your choice

Shortcut Key Lime Pie

Ingredients

- 1 carton (8 ounces) fat-free whipped topping
- 1 purchased or prepared graham cracker crust
- 1/4 cup boiling water
- 2 cartons (6 ounces each) Key lime yogurt
- 1 package (0.3 ounces) sugar-free lime gelatin

Directions

- In a mixing bowl, dissolve the gelatin in hot water
- Stir gelatin about two minutes until gelatin is completely dissolved.
- Whisk in yogurt.
- Gently fold in whipped topping.
- Pour into the filling into the crust.
- Using a spatula, level, and smooth the filling.
- Refrigerate, covered, until set, about 2 hours.
- Garnish, if desire
- Cut and serve cold.

Servings

- This recipe makes eight servings

Lavender Peach Puff Pastries

Ingredients

- 1 cup vanilla yogurt
- 1 sheet frozen puff pastry

- 3-4 fresh peaches or 1 15oz can sliced peaches
- Edible lavender
- Honey, for drizzling

Directions

- Preheat oven to 375F/190C.
- Cut the pastry sheet into 6 rectangles.
- Put the rectangles on a baking sheet.
- Put the baking sheet with the rectangles in the oven on the center shelf of the oven
- Bake for 3 minutes.
- Remove from heat and spread yogurt on top of each one. Layer with peaches and bake again 10 minutes or until pastry is puffed.
- Remove from oven, then drizzle with honey and sprinkle with lavender.

Servings

- This recipe makes 6 servings

Easy Fresh Peach Smoothie

Ingredients

- ½ cup milk of your choice
- ½ teaspoon ground cinnamon
- 1 fresh peach, pitted, chopped
- 1/3 cup vanilla yogurt or vanilla Greek yogurt
- Crushed ice, as required
- Sweetener of your choice to taste

Directions

- Combine all the ingredients in a blender.
- Pulse blend until smooth.
- Pass the smoothie mixture through a strainer if desired.
- Pour into a glass and serve.

Servings

- Makes 1 – 2 serving

Raspberry and Peach Smoothie

Ingredients

- 1 1/2 cups milk
- 1 cup fresh raspberries
- 1/2 cup plain Greek yogurt
- 2 peaches, pitted, chopped
- Ice cubes, as required

- Sweetener, sugar, honey, or agave nectar to taste

Directions

- Combine all the ingredients in a blender.
- Pulse blender until ingredients are smooth.
- Pour into 2 chilled drinking glasses and serve.

Servings

- Makes 2 servings

Strawberry Oatmeal Smoothie Recipe

Ingredients

- 1 1/2 cups of frozen strawberries
- 1 banana, cut into chunks
- 1 cup of whole milk or plain unsweetened yogurt
- 1 teaspoon of sugar or sweetener equivalent (optional)
- 1/2 cup of rolled oats
- 1/2 teaspoon vanilla extract (optional)

Directions

- Peel and slice a fresh banana
- Add all ingredients to blender and lock lid
- Pulse blend until well mixed and smooth
- Pour into two chilled glasses, garnish (if desired) and serve.

Servings

- About two eight-ounce glasses

Apple Smoothie

Ingredients

- ¼ cup milk
- ½ teaspoon honey
- 1 small apple, peeled (if desired), cored, chopped
- 2-3 almonds, chopped (optional)
- 3 tablespoons vanilla or plain yogurt
- A pinch ground cinnamon, to garnish (optional)
- Ice cubes (optional)

Directions

- Put all the ingredients and add them to a blender.
- Pulse blend until smooth.
- Pour into a glass.
- Garnish with cinnamon and serve.

Servings

- Makes 1 serving

Cook's notes

- The variety of Apple you choose to use will make a difference in how sweet or tart this smoothie is. If you like a sweeter smoothie Try an Apple-like the Honey Crisp if you like your smoothie a little more on the tart side, then try a Granny Smith.
- I recommend you wash the Apple thoroughly and use the Apple with the peal on, this makes the smoothie more nutritious, more colorful and prettier to look at.

Conclusion

Now, you have all the information to be 'yogurt expert.' Not only have you learned various methods of making different types of yogurt, but also accumulated enough information on how the process actually works. We made sure that along with showing you the right method with all the necessary details, you also have gotten to know how it works. You now also know that the yogurt world you envisioned for yourself isn't confined within your region but is widespread across different countries in the world. If you've already heard about or tasted every type of yogurt that has been mentioned in this book, then you know your yogurt extremely well. And if not, you must be intrigued to create or taste many—if not all—of them.

If you've been consuming store-bought yogurt all your life, we encourage you to stop doing that and start making your yogurt. It's cheap, healthy, and delicious. There are zero preservatives in it. Plus, you get to try a ton of recipes with the yogurt you made. If you have access to the specific types of cultures that were mentioned in this book, you can try creating yogurt types that are popular in specific regions. Trust us, some of those are super delicious.

And did we emphasize the benefits of yogurt enough? We know that it's rich in nutritional value with a high amount of protein and calcium, along with other vital constituents such as riboflavin, vitamin B12, potassium, magnesium, and certain other minerals. Plus, a significant benefit is that the bacteria and probiotics present in it are good for your gut health and help in improving digestion.

It's time to switch to healthier options and ditch those unhealthy products that contain harmful substances. And with such ease, there's no reason why you wouldn't want to start making your own yogurt at home.

Making Ayran

The healthy, refreshing, and tasty Turkish drink, Ayran, is straightforward to make with only three ingredients in a matter of minutes. Ayran is essentially a mix of water, yogurt, and salt, and lots of people considered it a great summer drink, for it is a refreshing beverage. It is also a right home make recipe since you can adjust the thickness and the taste of the yogurt to your liking.

Not only is Ayran inexpensive and straightforward to create, but it also brings many health benefits such as being a good source of calcium and protein. It also helps your digestive system and aid with your summer dehydration.

Ingredients

- 1 cup of cold water
- 2 cups of cold plain yogurt
- (Optional) Salt according to taste.

Equipment

- a blender or a mixing bowl and an immersion blenders/electric hand mixer
- drinking glasses

Directions

- Combine ingredients in a mixing bowl or blender jar
- Blend the mixture in a blender, an immersion blender, or electric hand mixer. If you don't have these machines, you can also put it in a sealed jar and shake it until it is smooth or have the texture of the yogurt.
- Pour into drinking glasses
- Garnish and serve chilled.

Printed in Great Britain
by Amazon